HL7 for Busy Professionals

Your No Sweat Guide to Understanding HL7

HL7 for Busy Professionals

Your No Sweat Guide to Understanding HL7

Rahul Bhagat
Illustration By Calvin Hui

Anchiove
2015

First Printing: 2015

ISBN 978-0-9939945-0-0

Anchiove Inc.
135 Wynford Dr., Toronto, ON, Canada M3C OJ4

www.HL7Book.com

To Neelam Bhagat,
who knew this book was for real before I did.
Thank you ma.

Contents

Preface

After university, I got a job with a busy, Toronto based, healthcare consulting company. On day two at work, I was handed a printout with cryptic text on it, and a document called interface spec, to read and understand. This was my introduction to HL7. At that time, I did not realize that this obscure messaging protocol would become my ticket to far off places, and the reason to meet and work with a lot of people.

It didn't take me long to learn HL7, my programming background helped. Later, I realized that my skill is in high demand and I became a consultant. I traveled to different cities and worked on various HL7 projects.

I also started running into people from non-technical background who wanted me to explain HL7 in the elevator or while chatting in their cubicle. There wasn't any introductory book I could suggest, so the idea of writing one myself.

I'm glad I collaborated with Calvin Hui in writing this book. He not only took care of illustration and design but also nudged me when I was slacking after the first draft. My friend Erik Westermann was a great sounding board and helped me refine my ideas. And thanks to many colleagues who helped me develop my skills. In particular, Derrick Leung, who mentored me when I was just starting out.

So here it is. My idea of an introductory book on HL7. I hope you enjoy reading it.

PART I

Scratching the surface

1. Introduction

A technical book usually implies a dry subject. So its no surprise authors have a hard time figuring out ways to make the book interesting to the reader. HL7 is one such subject. It is a subject that is so high on the scale of dryness and no one comes to it willingly. The only reason someone would read a book on HL7 is because of his or her job. And if you are here, reading this book, then I assume you work in healthcare IT or intend to join the industry soon.

I have made every effort to take out the dryness of the subject and make this book interesting. There are no needless jargons or esoteric concepts thrown casually to trip you. In fact, you will see a heavy reliance on everyday examples and inclusion of background information to paint a complete picture. But HL7 and healthcare system integration are complex subjects so there will be topics that don't make sense right away. Please persevere. Tie a knot and hang in there. Gradually things will make sense.

This introductory book on HL7 goes in detail to explain what HL7 is. It gives you the basic concepts, tells you about the organization behind it and helps you create a mental map of the voluminous HL7 specification document. And, it takes you through a whirlwind tour of some of the most commonly used HL7 messages, all in a short span of time.

Early Railroads

HL7 was created to solve the problems of clinical system integration. But to truly understand the problems of system integration, let's start with another integration problem we solved centuries ago.

The 1800's were a time when railways were coming of age in America – just like battery driven cars, drones and other new technologies are coming of age today.

There were literally hundreds of companies competing for a piece of the railway pie. Enterprising companies would buy up land, lay down tracks and run a transport service between cities which had no other means of transportation except for horse-drawn wagons or, if one was fortunate, steamships.

By the time American civil war started (1861), vast stretches of the continent were already connected through rail and work was well underway on the construction of the transcontinental railroad to connect California with the rest of the country.

However, there was one problem. You could not just hop on a train and get off at your destination, like you can today. Because these railroads were built and run by different companies, they used different track gauges (horizontal distance between two rails of the track). This meant you had to get off and change trains whenever you hit a junction with two different gauge widths. There were well over twenty different track gauges being used at the time of the civil war. The army had to constantly load and unload cargo in its effort to get supplies to the troops. This was a serious problem!

And it was the reason that finally made the American government to push for the conversion of all railway tracks to a standard gauge—4 feet and 8.5 inches, the most commonly used gauge width. More than half of the existing tracks were built to this width so it was easiest to convert the remaining tracks to this width and achieve standardization.

Standardization of rail tracks was the first step towards creating an integrated system where goods and people could move freely across the whole network. It was followed by the development of a common signal system, time zones, harmonized train schedule, fixed coach height, a standard coal and water supply system and on and on.

It was evident that an integrated system needed a standard way of doing things.

Evolution of Healthcare IT Systems

Today, we are in a (somewhat) similar situation with the movement of healthcare information. It cannot seamlessly flow from one system to the next. Each organization has its own way of storing and sharing information. Whenever health information needs to move across organization boundaries, it hits the incompatible standards roadblock. Someone has to unload and reload the information.

Healthcare IT systems have evolved similar to railroads. Initially, hardware costs (think multi-million dollar mainframes) were the biggest factor, so only a few teaching hospitals with deep pockets had the means to build a system. These were primarily stand-alone systems meant to serve a specific purpose. For example, to manage patient population in a large hospital.

Then the hardware cost came down and minicomputers arrived on the scene. A computer could be had for less than $25,000 and didn't need a room to house it. This allowed smaller players and even departments within a hospital to purchase systems of their own. Pharmacies installed systems to track prescriptions and dispensed medication while laboratories set up systems to track requests for tests and their results.

This led to dramatic improvement in productivity for these organizations but there was no free flow of information between the clinical systems. The problem was lack of standardization. Information from one system had to be unloaded to paper and transported to where the other system was. Then a human operator would reload the information to the other system by manually typing it in.

Of course this was the worse case scenario. Improvements were made. Information was loaded on floppy disks and electronically moved to the other system. Still, there was no free flow of information between systems. This prevented us from realizing the true potential of electronic systems.

Then some IT vendors came up with a solution. Replace stand-alone systems with an integrated product - an EHR (electronic health record). If you are familiar with Cerner, Epic or Meditech then you know what I am talking about. A large system with modules for every department.

This eliminated the need for health information to cross system boundaries. Within the system, the modules would use a standard way of storing and sharing information and this would allow the information to flow seamlessly within the organization.

This approach worked well. EHRs have been very successful in eliminating the problem of integrating systems within an organization and they continue to be one of the cornerstones of the healthcare IT structure.

But what about sharing information outside the organization? Healthcare organizations don't work in isolation. They need to share information with insurance companies and send patient care information to the government. They have to constantly communicate with the outside world.

To use our railway analogy, this was similar to the situation where each state could set its own standard gauge. You could travel all over a state without the need to switch trains but when you wanted to cross the state boundary, you would need to disembark and get on a train that ran on the other state's standard gauge.

Clearly, EHRs were only a limited solution.

There was also the question of what to do with existing standalone clinical systems. These systems were built over many years through substantial monetary investment. An organization would be loath to scrap all that investment & hard work and replace it with an EHR.

Healthcare needed a better solution. It needed a standard gauge to connect these EHRs, standalone systems, external systems and systems that were yet to be built. It needed to move away from constantly loading and unloading information.

The solution was HL7.

2. What is HL7?

HL7 is an ANSI accredited, OSI level 7, application layer protocol for exchanging clinical and administrative data between healthcare systems.

Chances are, if you are not a network engineer or did not study computer science, then *"OSI level 7, application layer protocol"* probably means nothing to you.

In lay terms, you can say that HL7 is a language that clinical systems use to exchange information with each other. But even that doesn't tell you anything. When I was learning HL7, the definition raised its own questions and left me with a vague sense of unease. It took a fair bit of research to figure out what HL7 is.

So instead of leaving with a sense of unease, why don't we take the time and figure out what HL7 really is?

Application Layer Protocol

HL7 is an application layer protocol. This means that it defines the rules for exchanging data (clinical and administrative) between applications.

We often use the word system and application in an informal way, which clouds the distinction between the two. Historically an application was the same as a system. An old accounting system, with its hardware and printers and monitors had only one job or application– preparing and maintaining financial records.

Things changed when systems became more powerful and started taking on multiple roles. A great example is your smartphone. It's not just a phone anymore. Making a phone call is just one of the many functions of the device. It has numerous "apps" or applications for all sorts of things.

Similarly, modern computer systems or servers run multiple applications, including clinical applications. When applications communicate with each other, they have to do so through their system. Basically, applications create a message in a language that is understood by their counterpart applications – in our case HL7 – and hand it over to their system for delivery. The system doesn't understand the message. Its job is to reliably deliver the message to the destination system.

HL7 is one such specialized application-to-application language/messaging rule book/protocol – whatever you call it – for communication between clinical applications.

OSI Level 7

HL7 is also an OSI (Open System Interconnection) Level 7 protocol. This is just a formal way of saying that it is an application layer protocol.

Now, we are going to discuss OSI and its levels and that means splashing through packet based, network communication. If you are not interested in it, I would suggest skipping over to the next chapter.

OSI is a reference model that networking guys use to make sense of the network communication model and how things really happen at the bit and byte level.

It is not difficult to understand the OSI model. The secret is proper background knowledge and an understanding of the key concepts. Let's see if we can do that in a few short pages here.

Historical Background

Using electricity for communication started with Samuel Morse, the inventor of the telegraph. He created a simple circuit with a battery, a bowl of mercury and two long wires grounded at ends.

If he dipped a wire in the bowl of mercury, it completed the circuit and current flowed through it. To send a short burst of electricity, he would dip the wire and pull it out quickly. This was like sending electric "smoke puffs" to the other end.

This basic idea was refined into the telegraph and Morse code. The code had two letters – a *dot* and a *dash*. A dot was a short puff of electricity and a dash was a longer puff (about 3 times the duration of a dot). Dots and dashes were combined to represent letters and voila! we had electronic communication.

> SOS, the universal distress signal, owes its origin to Morse code. In Morse code, the pattern for the letter **S** is three dots and for the letter **O**, it is three dashes - hence the familiar sound of three short beeps, three long beeps and three short beeps for SOS.

Morse code evolved into Baudet code for Teletypes, which replaced the dots and dashes with *bits*. Basically, instead of looking out for puffs of electricity, systems checked if current was flowing in a slice of time. This slice of time was called a bit. Each bit had two states; either current was flowing or not flowing. They used to call them a marking state and a spacing state. Today we know them as 1 and 0.

The time duration of a bit is called *bit time*. To understand bit time, let's assume a bit time of one second. If electricity was flowing for one second then that means a 1 was sent. If the electricity kept flowing during the next second then that means another 1. But, if there was no electricity after the first second, then that was a 0. In real life, bit times are extremely small. You can pack millions of bits in a second. This is also known as the bit rate (bits per second).

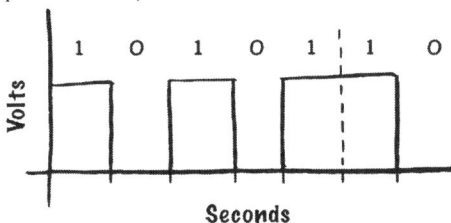

The success of electronic communication increased the need for communication lines for transmission. Back in the days, there were very few lines. So devices had to share lines to transmit their bits. The problem with this approach was that other devices had to wait until the transmitting device finished sending its message.

To give you an analogy, consider when we only had landlines. People had multiple handsets in the house but there was just one line. So if your teenage daughter was on the phone in her bedroom upstairs, you had better get busy doing whatever else you had to do. It would be a long time before it was your turn to make a call. Devices that had to share lines had a similar problem.

Packets

The solution was timesharing. The long stream of bits in a message was divided into smaller pieces called *packets*. Each computer on the network was given its share of time (say $1/100^{th}$ of a second) on a rotating basis and when its time came, it would transmit as many packets as it could. If all the packets were not sent in the allocated time, the computer would wait its turn to send the remaining packets. This way multiple computers were able to use the same transmission line without having to wait for an inordinate amount of time.

Message as a long stream of bits

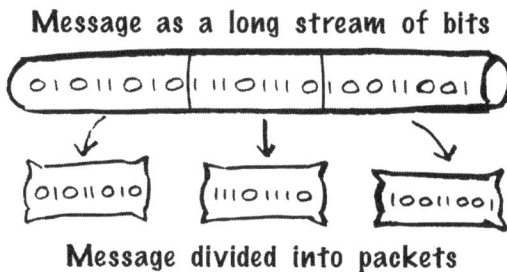

Message divided into packets

This method of message transmission has been so successful that today almost all communication is in the form of packets, even voice communication. If you have ever had a bad connection during a phone call, you may have noticed a number of gaps in the conversation. Those gaps were nothing but missing packets. They never made it in time!

For a message to be sent as packets requires a couple of things. One, the packets have to be numbered sequentially. If the packets are not assembled in the same order as they were sent, the message will become garbled. As a result, your thank you could end up before the hello.

And second, in a network with many computers, each packet will have to have the address of the destination computer. Otherwise where does the packet get delivered to?

These details are attached to a packet in the form of a header, as additional bits in front of the packet.

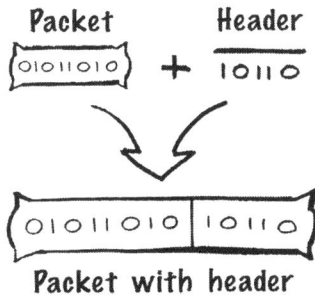

Packet with header

When the packet reaches its destination, the headers are stripped and the data is pieced together one by one to rebuild the original message.

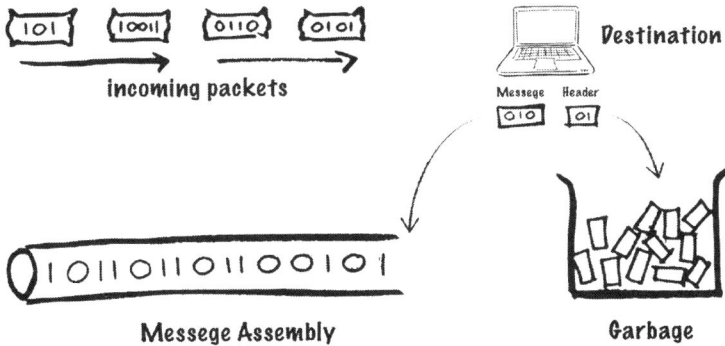

15

Ethernet

The Ethernet is the de-facto standard for connecting computers in a network. There were others, SNA, AppleTalk etc. but they didn't survive the Darwinian laws of free market.

To set up an Ethernet, you first lay down the communication backbone, which is a simple coaxial cable. The network is built by connecting individual devices to this backbone. If a device wants to send a message to another device (a computer, printer etc.) on the network, it transmits the packets to the backbone. Every device connected to the backbone will hear and read the header of the packet. If the packet is not addressed to it, it will be ignored. Only the device with the matching address will save the packet.

To assign a unique address to each device, an addressing system called MAC ID (Media Access Control ID) has been developed. It is a six-byte number, which is permanently stamped on every Network Interface Card (part of the device that connects to the network) by the manufacturer. That's why it is also called the hardware address or physical address. You cannot change it. It is permanently etched in the chip.

Packets carry this MAC ID in their header. When a device receives a packet, it compares the MAC ID of the packet with its own MAC ID. If it matches, it will store the packet, otherwise, it will ignore it. Once all the packets are received, the system stitches together the original message and sends it to the application for processing.

TCP/IP and the Internet

MAC ID works great for local networks where the administrator knows all the devices and their addresses. Communication breaks down when messages have to travel between networks. How are you going to find out the MAC ID of a computer on a far away network?

Back in the days, for American armed forces, this was a serious problem. Army, Navy and Air Force networks didn't have the capability to communicate with each other. Imagine the confusion in a theatre of war! But believe it or not, this was not the primary reason for the invention of the Internet. It was much more mundane. Computer science researchers were looking for a way to access supercomputers on other networks. There were only a few supercomputers around and if you were in San Diego and wanted to use the supercomputer at the University of California, Los Angeles, then your only recourse was to get on I5 and drive to LA.

So the researchers at ARPA (Advanced Research Projects Agency) created something called TCP/IP and used it to successfully connect four research networks, three in California and one in Utah, to each other. This first network of networks was called ARPANET. It was the acorn that grew into the massive oak tree we know today as the Internet.

So how did the folks at ARPA do it?

They created a system of virtual global addresses. Instead of using the MAC ID, which is fixed and burned on a device, they developed a virtual addressing system of four numbers where each number can have a value from 0 to 255, for example, 125.0.200.75. A device was assigned a unique combination of these four numbers, which became its global, unique IP (Internet Protocol) address.

If you are wondering how each device on the Internet gets a global unique IP address, then you should know that there is an entire organizational structure dedicated to the task. At the top is an organization called ICANN, based in LA, which does high-level coordination and decides on big things, such as, are we going to allow the xxx domain? Under it are five regional organizations that manage the actual allocation and assignment of IP numbers for their region.

The regional organizations are ARIN (North America), RIPE (Europe & Middle East), APNIC (Asia Pacific), LACNIC (Latin America & Caribbean) and AfriNIC (Africa).

If a network wants to connect to the Internet, it makes a request for a block of IP numbers to one of these organizations or their affiliates. Depending on the size of its network, it can get one of three classes of IP addresses: Class A, Class B or Class C.

For a large company like AT&T, which has a network with hundreds of thousands of devices and still needs room for more, a Class A block of addresses are assigned, for example, 12.x.x.x. All packets starting with the IP address 12 will go to AT&T's network, everything from 12.0.0.0 to 12.255.255.255. That's almost seventeen million addresses!

But if AT&T were smaller, it would receive a Class B block of addresses, for example, 12.200.x.x. In this case, all IP addresses from 12.200.0.0 to 12.200.255.255 would belong to the AT&T network.

For Class C addresses, the first three numbers are fixed, for example 12.200.50.x. All IP addresses between 12.200.50.0 and 12.200.50.255 belong to the network.

Once a network has its list of IP addresses, it creates an ARP (Address Resolution Protocol) table. An ARP table is nothing but a long list of physical addresses (MAC ID) of all the devices on the network and their corresponding IP addresses. With the help of this ARP table, the network can easily translate the IP address of an incoming packet to its corresponding MAC ID and vice versa.

This setup devised by ARPA freed the networks from the requirement of having to know each other's MAC IDs. For a device that wanted to communicate with the rest of the world, all it had to do was share its IP address. When the local network received a packet with this IP address, it would use the ARP table to find out the MAC ID of the device and attach it to the header of the packet before releasing it on its network.

If you are thinking why didn't they just use the MAC ID for addresses, keep in mind that there were already millions of devices out in the world before they started working on the problem. Cataloguing existing ID's and coordinating between manufacturers would have been a nightmare. It was easier to just start over with a clean slate.

To use this virtual address, when a packet is first created, a header with the IP address of the destination is attached to it. After that, another header with the MAC ID of the destination is added and then the packet is released on the Ethernet for transmission to the destination system.

If the destination is on the same network then there is no need for the IP address. The device with the matching MAC ID picks up the packet and strip away both the physical address (MAC ID) and the virtual address (IP) headers of the packet to get to the actual content.

Things are different when the message is for a device that is not on the local network.

After a packet is created and destination IP header attached, the local system looks up the ARP table to get the corresponding MAC ID of the destination. If the device is on a different network, then there will be no entry for it in the ARP table.

In that case, the physical address of a special device called a router is used. The packet is sent to the router on the network. The router reads the IP address of the destination and consults another table called the Forwarding Table, to determine where to send the packet on the Internet.

Forwarding tables are similar to ARP tables but instead of the physical address of local devices, they contain addresses of routers and gateways for other networks. If the destination network is known then the packet is sent directly to it, otherwise it gets sent to the gateway, which is like a central post office.

From there it gets bounced around the world, based on a host of factors, till it reaches its destination network.

The router at the destination network uses the IP address of the packet to find the corresponding physical address in its ARP table. It then adds the corresponding physical address header to the packet and releases it on its local network, where the destination device with matching MAC ID picks it up for processing.

This is how ARPA was able to connect different networks and usher in the Internet age.

Layers

If you noticed, with Internet there were two headers added to every packet, which allowed it to travel between networks. One was the virtual address header (IP) and the second was the physical address header (MAC ID). In techie speak, the packets passed through two *layers* where these headers were added. Layers can be seen as process steps that transform a packet.

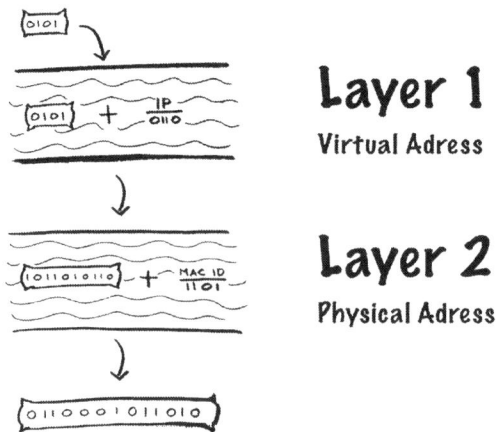

Layer 1
Virtual Adress

Layer 2
Physical Adress

If you recall the discussion at the beginning of the chapter, communication between two applications is independent of the underlying system. The system does not understand the message. It only facilitates the movement of messages from one application to the other.

But this system level facilitation is not just taking a message, chopping it into packets and passing them down the wire to the other system. There is more to it and we saw some of that. The packets had two address headers attached to them. In the real world there are many other things that can happen to a packet before it is sent down the wire.

For example, a message can be compressed before it is sent or it can be encrypted before it is transmitted.

For a better understanding of the message transformation process let's compare it to an automobile assembly line. Before a car rolls off the assembly line, its chassis passes through a number of workstations or stops. At each stop, it undergoes a transformation. First the chassis is welded, then the paint job is done, then the dashboard is put in place, the seats are assembled, and so on.

Similarly, before a message is transmitted down the wire, it passes through a number of stops or what technical folks like to call *layers*. At each layer the message undergoes a transformation.

Very often there are multiple ways of transformation. At the welding stop, you can choose between gas welding or arc welding or even laser welding for something really precise. Similarly, there are different methods for transforming a message at each layer. Technical folks like calling them *protocols*.

These are the fundamental concepts in network communication. Packets that travel on the Internet today go through many layers that implement all kinds of functionality. At each layer, there could be many different protocols to bring about the desired transformation.

To take an example, the researchers at ARPA also wanted to make sure that if a packet was lost during transmission, there was a process to resend it. To achieve this, they added another layer before the virtual address layer to ensure guaranteed delivery of each packet.

This new layer was the transport layer. It added another header with a tracking number to the packet. When the destination system received the packet, it was required to send back a short acknowledgement with the original tracking number of the packet.

This way the source system was able to figure out which packets were received by the destination. If a packet was lost, there would be no acknowledgement for it. After waiting for a couple of seconds the source system would automatically resend that packet.

But not every application wanted guaranteed delivery of packets. For some applications, packets have to be delivered in real time. Think of video conferencing or streaming radio. If a packet is lost, it's lost. For these applications, techies developed a different protocol, called UDP, which only cared about sending the packets in sequence, in real time. If a packet didn't arrive on time, too bad, that will be a blip, we are moving to the next packet.

Eventually, this led to a proliferation of protocols. There were protocols for Internet chat, protocols for peer-to-peer file sharing, protocols for Internet telephony and on and on. People were building all kinds of crazy things and someone needed to step in and bring order to the situation.

Open Systems Interconnection (OSI) Model

The anarchy with the protocols prompted the international standards setting organization to try and bring some order to the chaos. Academics huddled together and came up with a clean, seven level framework for network communication called Open Systems Interconnection (OSI). It divided the process of sending and receiving messages into seven levels (steps) and defined which actions can be performed at each level.

Level	
7	**Application Layer:** At this layer, data to be sent is organized in a message according to the structure and rules of the application protocol. (e.g. HL7)
6	**Presentation Layer:** At this layer, work like encryption and compression of data is carried out. Large files like video and image use this layer.
5	**Session Layer:** At this layer, functionality can be added to maintain an ongoing conversation without having to confirm the identity of the system for every message. Other functionalities like voice and video synchronization can also be added.
4	**Transport Layer:** This is the layer where the sending system divides the message into packets and the receiving system reassembles them. Tracking and acknowledgement of packets is also done at this level. A commonly used protocol for this layer is TCP.
3	**Network Layer:** At this layer, a virtual address (IP) is added to the packet. The IP protocol is for this layer.
2	**Data Link Layer:** This is the layer where a physical address is added to the packet. This is where the MAC ID is added.
1	**Physical Layer:** This layer transmits the 0s and 1s of the packet as electric pulses down the wire. For cell phones the signal travels as microwaves and for fiber optic cables it is a pulse of light.

The messaging process starts with the application layer or level 7 of the OSI model. After the transformation, the message is passed to level 6, which does its transformation and passes it further down the levels until the message reaches level 1. At this point the packet gets converted to 0's and 1's and is transmitted down the wire.

At the receiving end, the packet undergoes a reverse transformation. It starts at level 1 and moves to upper levels until it reaches level 7. At that point, the message is handed to the receiving application, which processes and consumes the message.

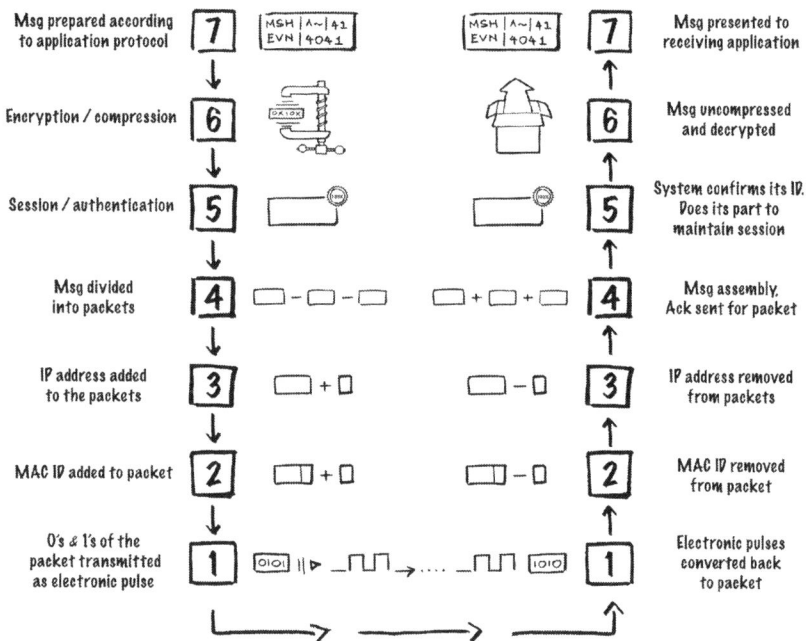

Msg prepared according to application protocol	**7**	**7**	Msg presented to receiving application
Encryption / compression	**6**	**6**	Msg uncompressed and decrypted
Session / authentication	**5**	**5**	System confirms its IP. Does its part to maintain session
Msg divided into packets	**4**	**4**	Msg assembly, Ack sent for packet
IP address added to the packets	**3**	**3**	IP address removed from packets
MAC IP added to packet	**2**	**2**	MAC IP removed from packet
0's & 1's of the packet transmitted as electronic pulse	**1**	**1**	Electronic pulses converted back to packet

By creating this seven-level model of network communication, the standards committee expected everyone to adopt OSI and establish it as the standard. Unfortunately, that's not how it turned out in real life.

By the time OSI was developed, TCP (for guaranteed delivery) and IP (virtual addresses for communication on Internet) were well entrenched in the networking world. Together the TCP/IP combo was sufficient to ensure transmission of packets over the Internet. As a result, organizations just added layers for application-to-application communication and other features as needed, and didn't bother conforming to the OSI model.

Still, OSI has survived as a good reference model for understanding network communication. Many protocols have been developed and continue to be developed which implement the functionalities of a specific level. The protocol can just say that it conforms to a particular level of the OSI model and everyone will know the functionality it implements.

Health Level 7 (HL7)

Health Level 7 is one such specialized protocol that conforms to level 7 of the OSI model. It is an application layer protocol, specifically created for communication between healthcare applications. So whenever there is a need to exchange health data between applications, guess which protocol is going to be used? HL7 of course.

Accepted, the name Health Level 7 is not exactly a friendly name. But if you look at it from the perspective of the people who developed it, you can see why they named it Health Level 7. It is an application layer protocol, which corresponds to level 7 of the OSI model. And the protocol is for the exchange of health information, hence the name, Health Level 7. I would argue that the name makes a lot of sense.

HL7 conforms to the OSI model but it only defines the protocol for seventh level. For other levels, the implementer is free to choose any combo of protocols. Usually MLLP (Minimum Lower Layer Protocol) with TCP/IP is used to implement lower level functionalities.

3. Integration Concepts

From a technical perspective, the word integration means to connect different systems (and applications) together. When systems are integrated, they can communicate with each other and exchange information.

This automatic flow of information is the reason we integrate systems. Because when systems are able to share information, it leads to a lot of benefits. One such very important benefit is maintenance of data consistency between different systems. Let me elaborate.

A big issue with isolated systems is creation of data silos. Over a period of time, a system will accumulate a mountain of clinical information in its database. But that database is only for its exclusive use. The information is locked away. This limits the usefulness of the data. Others, who need that data, have to copy it and maintain a separate database. Over time, the data becomes inconsistent in the copies, and this leads to unwanted headache.

Consider a stand-alone lab system that keeps a perfect record of tests ordered and their corresponding results. Since the information is locked away in the lab system, a physician who needs that information will receive a print out of the result. That paper result will eventually get filed away in that patient's folder for future reference.

So far so good. Both the lab system and the doctor's office have the same information. But what happens if there is a correction to the lab test? The lab system will update its database and also send a paper copy to the doctor's office. What happens if a staff member forgets to file it or the report is misplaced or ends up somewhere else?

The point is, there are endless ways for data to become inconsistent between systems. An integrated system avoids this situation by automatically exchanging information with other systems whenever there is new data to be shared or an existing data element changes.

Another benefit of integration is the ability to automate business processes. Systems don't just have to talk one-on-one. They can also be part of an information assembly line where one system takes the order, another checks the validity of the credit card, and yet another coordinates shipment of the order. Integration allows for automatic movement of relevant information from one system to the next and this makes business process automation very simple.

HL7 and the healthcare industry are late to the game of business process automation. The granddaddy protocol is EDI (Electronic Data Interchange), which is one of the oldest and most widely used standard for data integration. It is now primarily used by the retail/manufacturing industry. Banks and other financial organizations have a standard of their own, called SWIFT, which takes into account their need for ultra-high accuracy and security.

And finally, the ability to integrate systems gives us a better method to create large aggregate systems without having to worry about the doomsday scenario - the day when a large, monolithic system crashes down. By stringing together smaller, independent systems through message-based integration, we can isolate them from each other and minimize the impact a particular system can have on the entire ecosystem. To use our example from before, if the order delivery system goes down, it will delay order shipment but the organization is still open for business and accepting orders - probably with a warning that shipments could be delayed.

Synchronous and Asynchronous Communication

There can be two types of communication between integrated systems - synchronous and asynchronous.

Synchronous communication takes place just like a conversation. It happens in real time and uses the request/response model. One system will ask a question and the other system will respond with an answer. It is like making a phone call. You pick up the phone, dial the number, and say hello. Then you wait for the other end to respond.

Asynchronous communication is more like a text message. You type and send the message and get on with whatever else you were doing. You are not waiting for the other person to respond. This is a better and more efficient way to deal with situations where having the information immediately is not necessary.

Imagine a person showing up at the registration desk of a hospital. He has been feeling a tingling sensation in his feet that keeps coming back and he would like to see a doctor. The registration clerk asks for the man's information, including his insurance information, and creates a patient record. The next step is confirmation with the insurer before an appointment is scheduled with the doctor. This step is a perfect candidate for using synchronous communication to integrate the hospital system with the insurance company's system. It is necessary for the hospital system to confirm insurance details before an appointment is scheduled.

Well, finally the man gets to see the doctor. It could be nothing. But the doctor notices that he is overweight. He also has high blood pressure, and there are blisters on his feet. This gets the doctor concerned and she orders a blood test for sugar level and A1C to check if the patient has diabetes.

Here the synchronous communication method to integrate the hospital system with the lab system will not work. Blood has to be drawn, labeled, and shipped to the lab. This will take time. The order can be sent electronically immediately but neither the hospital system nor the lab system will, or should, keep waiting till the test results are available. This is where asynchronous communication is used to integrate systems.

Connection

How systems are physically connected is another important topic in integration. If there are only two systems, then there is no issue. You can connect them directly - point A to point B. This is a point-to-point connection.

A point-to-point connection works fine as long as the number of systems to be connected is low. And by low, we mean two or three. Anything higher and it starts becoming a serious issue. How? Read on.

For a system to be able to send messages to every other system on the network, it has to have a connection to every other system. To connect two systems, we only need a single connection between them. With three systems (A, B, and C), we will need three connections - A to B, B to C, and C to A.

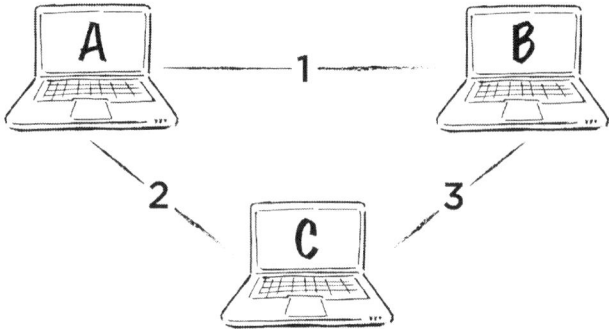

For four systems, the number of connection jumps to six. For five it is ten, six systems require fifteen connections and... ten systems require forty-five connections!

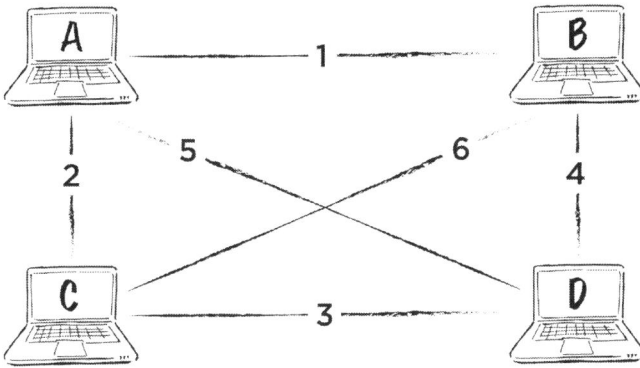

I did not have to manually count the number of connections for ten systems because there is a mathematical formula for it. Number of connections = $[(n/2) * (n-1)]$ where n is the number of systems. No matter how much you hate them, formulas have their usefulness.

You can see how this problem seriously limits the number of systems we can have in a network.

Well, it was not the first time we faced this problem. Transportation systems faced this issue long before computers and they solved it with the help of the hub-and-spoke model.

Delta Airlines pioneered the hub-and-spoke model back in the 1950s. Their merger with Chicago and Southern Airlines meant they had to create a network that integrated many more cities. They did this by coming up with the idea of an airline hub in Atlanta. One set of planes would ferry passengers to Atlanta and another to the final destination. Today, almost all airlines operate on this model, although, there are exceptions like SouthWest Airlines, which only flies point-to-point.

The company that really turned this model into an art was FedEx. To guarantee overnight package delivery, not only between San Francisco and New York City but also between Albany and El Paso, they set up a central clearinghouse in Memphis (their hub) and implemented the hub and spoke model for overnight package delivery.

All overnight packages are flown from various destinations to Memphis where incoming packages are sorted with the help of a high-tech conveyor belt system. The sorting is done within a four-hour window according to the destination location and at 2:50 AM, the first plane leaves Memphis for its destination. For the next hour (probably longer now) a plane takes off every minute to another destination. I would love to watch this symphony of modern age. Someday, maybe.

The hub-and-spoke model solved the problem of exponentially increasing connections in computer systems by using a hub in the network. If A wanted to send a message to Z, it sent that message to the hub, which in turn passed it on to Z. This way, the number of connections was equal to the number of systems. In other words, to connect ten systems, we only needed ten connections.

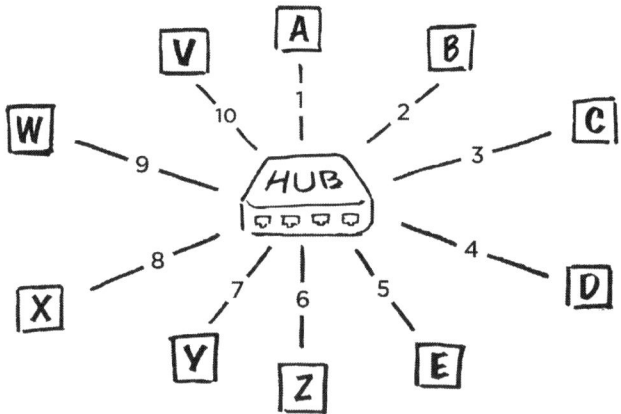

Publish-Subscribe Model

Using a hub to connect systems has other advantages. One such advantage is optimization of message generation from the source system to the destination.

Consider the case where system A has to send messages to systems B and Z. One option is that system A creates two identical copies of each message and sends one to B and the other one to Z. Under a different approach, system A creates only one message and sends it to the hub. Other systems that want to receive messages from A let the hub know that.

So, when the hub receives a message from A, it checks its instructions and notes that systems B and Z want to receive messages from A. It then creates two copies of the message and sends them to both the destination systems.

This is the publish-subscribe model of message routing. It not only reduces the number of messages and traffic on the network, it also frees up sending systems (like A) from having to keep track of who wants to receive what. This becomes the job of the hub.

The hub is very important in integration. You must have come across software like eGate, BizTalk, or Rhapsody. They are a class of software products called integration engines. At their heart, these products are hubs which route messages between systems on the network.

Message Triggers

Message triggers are real-life events that trigger generation of a message by a system. There are two situations.

One, it can be a *service request*. This is the request/ response model we discussed in the section on synchronous communication. For example, a doctor's office makes a service request to the lab system for an old test result. The lab system responds with a message that contains details of the old test result.

The second situation is *event notification*. Here a real world event triggers automatic generation of a message. For example, the lab system will generate an event-notification message when the result of a new test becomes available. Ordering systems don't have to keep asking if the result is available.

Scope of HL7

System integration is a vast topic. HL7 only occupies a small niche in healthcare system integration and exchange of healthcare data.

Even within healthcare system integration, HL7 doesn't set the standard for everything. If you divide it broadly, there are three standards that are required for integration: a message-transfer standard (how a message will be sent), a message-format standard (what a message will look like), and a data standard (how healthcare information will be organized in a message).

We saw in the last chapter how the Internet and TCP/IP protocol can be used to send messages between applications. HL7 does not reinvent the wheel. It leaves message-transfer standard to implementers. They can either use the Internet and TCP/IP or a dedicated network and their own custom protocol. HL7 doesn't care.

What HL7 does care about and defines standards for, are the message-format standards and data standards.

Message Format Standard

The message-format standard defines the structure of a message so that the receiving system can make sense of its content. If the data is not organized in a standard way then the system won't know where to look for it in the message. In that case, along with the message, the sending system will also have to send information about where to look for data and what each value means. That will be a very inefficient way of communicating.

If the same were true in our everyday life, then every speed limit sign on the highway will have to be a large descriptive board. This will be required because instead of just saying "*Max 100 km/hr.*", it will have to say, "*The vehicle you are operating on this stretch of the highway is not allowed to exceed the speed limit of 100 km per hour. This is against the law and if you are caught you will be penalized.*"

The point is, with a standard message format, you can have a short, to-the-point message, which is understood by everyone.

By defining a standard-message format, HL7 allows clinical systems to exchange short messages without them having to grapple with explaining the meaning of each field, every time they send a message.

Data Standard

Data standards deal with how information is represented in a message. It might seem like a simple thing but real tragedies have occurred because we mixed up the measuring unit (remember Mars orbiter?). By defining a comprehensive data standard, HL7 ensures that there is no ambiguity in the information that is shared between systems.

To illustrate, let's consider the simple example of the patient name field. A hospital system stores a patient's name in three different fields: first name, middle name and last name. In contrast, a lab system stores the patient's name in just one field with space between each part of the name.

These two systems cannot be integrated unless they agree on a common data standard. If the hospital sends the patient's name as is, the lab system will need an extra layer of software to stitch the name fields together and then save it to its database. And a patient's name is just one field. There could be thirty or forty fields in a message. Can you imagine the enormity of work involved in reconciling those fields? It would be a nightmare.

HL7 solves the problem by defining standard data format. If two systems want to integrate, then both of them will have to use the HL7 data standard for messaging. This way there will be no ambiguity with field content and there will be no need to undergo the laborious process of reconciling fields every time two systems are integrated.

4. Evolution of HL7

We live in a world of standards. As new technologies emerge, a necessary condition for their wide adoption is standardization. We notice it when there is a problem with the standard. As must be evident to anyone in a foreign country not able to plug in a laptop because the power outlet is different.

Standards emerge from different sources. A standard could be imposed by the government, as was the case with the conversion from the imperial to the metric system of measurement. Both the USA and Canada started the conversion but in the States, the government defunded the Metric Board, stalling their conversion. In Canada however, the conversion was completed and we started measuring distance in kilometers and temperature in Celsius.

Another source of standard is the industry itself. Companies at the forefront of a new technology vie for competitive advantage by promoting adoption of their technology. We have all heard about the famous videotape standards battle between Betamax and VHS. Sony's Betamax was a superior technology but VHS became the standard because JVC was relentless in promoting it to electronics manufacturers.

A third source of standard is market forces, which leads to a de-facto standard. This was the case with TCP/IP. It became the dominant, and ultimately standard, network-communication protocol as a result of gradual adoption by universities and businesses. By the time the ISO model was developed, it was too late for a switchover. TCP/IP was already baked in.

And finally, there is the deliberate approach where experts get together with the specific intent of creating a standard. This is how the HL7 standard came into being.

Development of HL7

The story of HL7 started in 1987. An international group of experts got together to work on the problem and created a rudimentary version of what we know today as HL7. It had many gaps and was not detailed enough for practical use, but it got the ball rolling.

A dedicated, not for profit organization called Health Level Seven International was founded to manage ongoing development of the standard.

The organization is completely volunteer driven. It draws its members from healthcare providers, vendors, consultants, government groups and others who have an interest in the development of standards.

Within a couple of years of its formation, it had the first usable version of HL7 (v2.1) ready, which was released in 1990. This was followed by a revised version (v 2.2) in 1994.

Industry adoption of HL7 was not very successful initially, but the user base kept growing slowly. The turning point came in 1997 when version 2.3 was released. This version was ANSI approved which signaled to the industry that the standard was robust and mature.

ANSI approval was like a shot in the arm for HL7. Adoption accelerated and picked up further pace with the release of version 2.3.1 in 1999. This led to much broader market recognition, wider industry adoption, and eventually to the current status as the dominant industry standard for the exchange of clinical and administrative health information.

ANSI (American National Standards Institute)

ANSI is a private, not-for-profit organization in the United States, which facilitates, coordinates and oversees standards development activities. ANSI itself doesn't develop any standards, it only defines guidelines and a process for standard development. If another organization, like HL7, follows the guidelines and process to develop its standard then it gets ANSI approval.

The ANSI process is a consensus-driven standard development process. The idea is to ensure that no single party dominates and every interested party has an opportunity to voice its opinion. It also requires standard development to be conducted in an open environment under public scrutiny.

ANSI approval is granted for five years with an additional five years extension if requested. At the end of the approval period, the standard is reviewed to determine if it should be reapproved, revised, or withdrawn.

HL7 Organizational Structure

A board of directors, composed of elected and appointed members, oversees the development of HL7 standard. The organization also has numerous technical committees and special interest groups (SIG), made entirely of volunteers. They are the ones who develop and revise the standards. Each technical committee or SIG has two or more co-chairs who manage the work within the group. Together, co-chairs from all the groups form the Technical Steering Committee, which is the clearinghouse for new and revised standards. Once the Technical Steering Committee votes and agrees to a new standard, it is sent to the board of directors, which makes the final decision on releasing the standard to general audience.

Anyone can volunteer and get involved in the development of HL7 standards. All one needs to do is become a member of HL7.org or its affiliate (if outside the USA) and then register with one of the active work groups.

Versions of HL7

Since the release of the first version of HL7 in 1987, the organization has made regular revisions of the standard.

With each new version, the standard has been improved by adding new rules, modifying existing rules, or by finding solutions to issues raised by the implementers. It has also been necessary to ensure that each new version is backward compatible. In other words, a new version is able to communicate with systems using older versions of the standard.

Backward compatibility adds a lot of legacy burden and makes it much more difficult to improve a standard. We saw what a quirky task it is with the release of Windows 8. Users of Windows operating system were used to the start button to run applications. When Windows 8 came out with a revamped user interface where instead of using the start button, users were presented with tiles to run the applications, all hell broke loose. Microsoft had to quickly release version 8.1 and bring back the start button to keep its customer base happy.

Similarly, HL7 has had to ensure that with each new version, the old structure and format is not disturbed. Version 2.1 of HL7 was the first implementable version and since its release there has been eight revisions of the standard: v2.2, v2.3, v2.3.1, v2.4, v.2.5, v2.5.1, v2.6 and v2.7. Of these, HL7 v2.3 and v2.3.1 are the most widely implemented versions. They account for over three quarters of all HL7 messages.

All versions are compatible with each other. If an older-version message is sent to a system using a new version, the system will still be able to read the message. Similarly, a system compatible with an older version will be able to read a newer version message by ignoring additional features present in the message.

But there are serious problems with this approach. To maintain backward compatibility, HL7 has had to leave many attributes optional and allow a lot of room for customization. This has prompted some to even call HL7 a non-standard standard. The problem is that you cannot just send an HL7 message to any system. Every time two systems need to communicate, a unique HL7 interface has to be created with all the options and customization involved.

HL7 Version 3

To address these issues, it became necessary to break from the past and build a standard from the ground up. The result is HL7 v3.0, which was first released in 2005. The version number no longer changes with this new form of HL7, but it is revised annually. HL7 v3.0 exists alongside HL7 v2.x but they are not compatible. Incompatibility between v2.x and v3.0 means that systems implementing v3.0 interfaces will not be able to communicate with systems implementing v2.x messages. Although not impossible, it takes considerable time and effort to convert v2.x messages to v3.0 and because of that, the adoption of v3.0 is still very low.

HL7 v3.0 is being implemented in places where there are little or no existing systems. Governments in Europe have used v3.0 to create new healthcare networks, and in Canada, v3.0 adoption is being driven by the federal and provincial governments' initiative to create drug-information networks and registries of healthcare providers. In the United States, the CDC has implemented some networks with v3.0 messaging, but overall the adoption remains low.

Given the widespread adoption of v2.x and its incompatibility with v3.0, it will be a long time before v3.0 replaces it as the dominant standard. And even then, v2.x will exist long into the future. If it ain't broken, organizations are not going to fix it. My first job was production support of an S/390 IBM mainframe. Its software code was written in COBOL in the 60's. No one is going to replace that code as long as it does its job.

Other Healthcare Standards

People working in healthcare IT know that HL7 is not the only standard they have to deal with. X12, SNOMED, ICD-9/10, DICOM, there are a lot of standards vying for their attention.

Generally speaking, most standards have been developed for a particular healthcare area such as medical imaging or insurance or for some kind of classification. Although HL7's area is clinical and administrative data, it can handle the messaging requirements (internal and external) of an entire organization. This distinguishes it from other standards, which are primarily focused on the needs of a particular area.

Take the example of DICOM (Digital Imaging and Communications in Medicine). It is the standard used by PACS and other imaging systems to transmit, retrieve, and store medical images. But DICOM can only be used between imaging systems. If a different system needs an image, it will have to be translated or embedded within an HL7 message.

Similarly, the X12N standard is used only for transmitting patient insurance and financial data to the insurance company. If additional patient information has to be sent, an HL7 message containing the information will have to be embedded within the X12N message.

Then there are standards just for classification, which have nothing to do with messaging.

ICD-9/10 (International Classification of Diseases) is a standard that clinicians use to classify diseases, injuries and causes of death. Revision 10 is the most current version, which also includes codes for classifying health-risk factors (occupational, environmental, lifestyle etc.). ICD codes are regularly sent as data elements in HL7 messages.

LOINC (Logical Observation Identifier Names and Codes) is a standard for classifying lab orders and tests. In this system, every possible lab test has a unique, three to seven digit ID number. An HL7 order message will only need to have this unique ID in its "ordered test" field for the receiving system to know which test has been ordered. Similarly, when the result is sent back, LOINC codes are used to specify the test that the result is for.

LOINC has more than seventy thousand codes. Each code corresponds to a different kind of lab test. For example, there is a test called Serum Sodium or Blood Sodium Level or Sodium-Blood, depending on who you are talking to. Its LOINC code is 2951-2. When this code is sent in an order message, the receiving system knows exactly that the test is to measure the concentration of salt in the blood. It is unambiguous and does away with the confusion of different names. If you have had a lot of salty food, your reading for 2951-2 will be north of 140. (The normal range is 135–145).

Then there is SNOMED-CT (Systematized Nomenclature of Medicine-Clinical Terminology), which is like a thesaurus for medical terms, diseases, anatomy and procedures. It uses ConceptID and DescriptionID to define codes, synonyms, and descriptions of medical terms. For example, myocardial infarction is a concept (ConceptID 22298006), which refers to infraction (death of tissue) in the myocardium (muscular wall of the heart).

These standards take you deep into the clinical world. If you not queasy about syringes and scalpels and stitches then keep wandering. For me this much information was more than enough and I never had any issues with these standards. As long as you have a rough idea what the content of a field represents, there won't be any problem working with these standards.

This brings us to the end of part I. We have covered the background information and now it's time to look at the standard itself. Even if you only read the next two or three chapters, it will give you a fairly good idea of the standard.

PART II

Digging Deeper

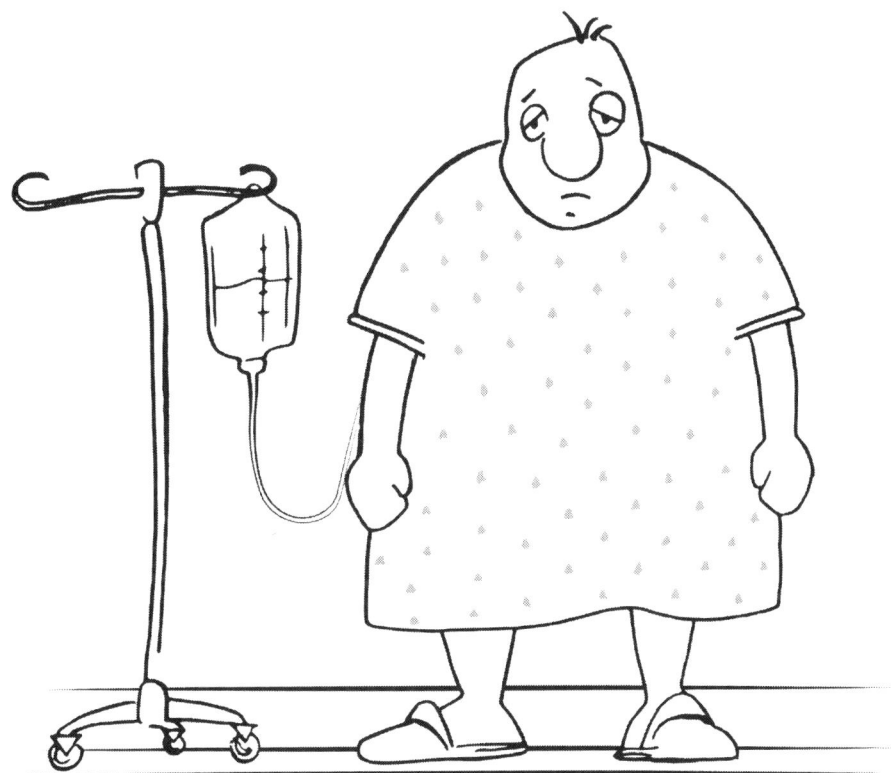

5. Basic Concepts

So now you understand that HL7 is an application layer (level 7) protocol that clinical systems use for sharing information. Also, because of a lot of optional elements and customization, HL7 is almost a non-standard standard. We can't just send any HL7 message to a system and expect it to understand the message.

When two or more systems are integrated, they have to first agree on the types of messages that will be exchanged and triggers events that will be supported. All this information (and more) is then documented in an *Interface Specification* document before actual work begins to integrate the systems.

If you have an environment where HL7 messages are used, then all this information on message type, trigger events, acknowledgement etc. is there somewhere in the form of one or more interface specification document.

You will need a good idea of some basic HL7 concepts before you are comfortably able to navigate these documents and other HL7 related artifacts. In the following pages we will cover these basic concepts.

Unsolicited Messages

HL7 messages are generally unsolicited. Not always, but in the vast majority of cases. Before we get to why most messages are unsolicited, let's see what kind of a beast an unsolicited message is.

Un-solicited or not solicited is the opposite of solicited. The word *solicit* means "to ask for something from someone". So its opposite, unsolicited, will probably mean "getting something from someone without asking for it".

I remember Toronto's Mayor Rob Ford landing in hot water while soliciting donation for his private football foundation. He was using City of Toronto letterhead for the purpose, not realizing you can't use the power of the office to *solicit* donation.

Similarly, if a system explicitly asks another system for a message, then that is soliciting. Messages in this case are solicited messages.

A database query is a good candidate for solicited messages. If you want to know the number of inpatient admissions for the day, the information is solicited as a query to the system, which responds with a message containing the number of admissions for the day.

Now imagine a world where all HL7 messaging is like this. After placing an order for a lab test, the system in the doctor's office will keep pestering the lab system for the test result. If the result is not ready, there is nothing the lab system can do. It doesn't have the information. This is an inefficient way of communicating that wastes processing power, degrades performance and is a real annoyance – like kids in the backseat constantly asking "Are we there yet?"

The alternative is an unsolicited message. In this case, the Lab system automatically sends the test result when it becomes available. It doesn't require the system placing the order to keep asking for the result. By placing an order, the system has implicitly indicated that it wants the result. Or in other words, it receives the result as an unsolicited message.

This is a much better way of communicating. It is an optimal solution where a message is created only when it is needed. And for that reason, most HL7 messages are unsolicited messages.

Message Type

While working with HL7 you will come across statements like, "this is an ADT message" or "we can process an Order message". These references, ADT and Order, are simply different message types. Message types are used in HL7 to group and classify similar messages.

If you are thinking HL7 message types are probably based on real world organization of a healthcare environment, then this is a good time to throw out that idea.

Instead of mirroring real world, HL7 message types are organized by their function. Take the example of an order message. It doesn't matter if the message is for a lab or a pharmacy, as long as the message is an order for something, a test, a medication or even housekeeping, it is an order message type. Similarly messages that deliver results, be it a lab test result, an X-Ray or an ultrasound, they are all result message types.

HL7 defines thirteen different kinds of message types but you don't really have to know them all. Real life usage of HL7 follows the 80-20 rule of the Pareto principle (example, 80% of accidents are caused by 20% of drivers or 80% of sales come from 20% of customers). Likewise, most HL7 messages use only a few of the message types available. Most healthcare organizations use only this small subset of message types and if you become familiar with the top three or four, you will have covered between sixty and seventy percent of real world implementations.

So what are these most commonly used message types?

As you know, HL7's area is clinical and administrative data. So it is no surprise that the most commonly used message type is *patient-administration.* This is the message type that groups together messages that have anything to do with managing a patient - admitting, discharging, updating their information, transferring to another unit etc.

The next two most commonly used message types, in my experience, are *Order Entry* (orders) messages and *Observation Reporting* (results) messages. But of course this can vary from place to place.

Another thing to know about message types is the *Message Type Code*. This is a three-character code that is used as an acronym for the message type. For patient-administration, there is just one code: ADT (short for Admission, Discharge and Transfer). All patient-administration messages are ADT messages.

For order-entry (orders), there are a few different message type codes, depending on the type of order the message is carrying. The code ORM is for the general order message. Although it has been discontinued in newer versions of HL7, ORM continues to be heavily used in older implementations. In addition to ORM, there is OML for lab orders, OMI for imaging order, OMD for dietary order and so on.

The observation-reporting (results) message type has a couple of different message type codes as well, but the code ORU is the one that is most commonly used. The code OUL has something to do with lab system automation and not used much. We won't waste our time on it.

The HL7 specification document (HL7 spec) is organized by message types. If you want to know more about a particular message type and its codes, all you have to do is flip to the chapter for that message type.

Trigger Event

HL7 messages are trigger-event driven. What does that mean? It means that an HL7 message is created only when something happens (an event) in the real world. This "something" in the real world is the trigger that sets the wheels in motion.

For example, admitting a patient is a real world event that triggers the creation of an HL7 message. When the hospital staff completes the admit form and hits enter, it sets off a chain reaction in the registration system that leads to the creation of the HL7 message. The content of the message depends on the event that triggered the message creation. In this case, it contains details of the patient being admitted.

Not every event in the real world triggers message creation. HL7 defines specific real world events within the context of a message type that can trigger message creation. It is these events that are called *trigger events*.

There is a long list of trigger events that map to real world events. For instance, ADT defines over sixty different trigger events. But this is a bit of an outlier because other message types don't have so many trigger events.

Even with so many trigger events, there could still be a situation where a message needs to be generated for a real world event that doesn't have a corresponding trigger event. In such cases, one will need to get a little creative and re-purpose another close enough trigger event for the situation.

Just like message types, trigger events have their own three-character *Trigger Event Code*. But there is a difference. Message-type codes are all uppercase letters whereas for trigger-event codes, the first character is a letter and the next two characters are numbers, such as A01 (patient admit) or A02 (transfer patient).

Together, a message type and a trigger event uniquely define an HL7 message. It is generally written by joining together the message-type code and trigger-event code with a caret (^) symbol. So, a patient admit HL7 message is represented as ADT^A01. A patient transfer HL7 message is represented as ADT^A02 and so on. Often people drop ADT and just refer to the messages as A01 or A02.

When two systems are being integrated, it is decided beforehand which HL7 messages will be sent. Let's say a hospital is implementing a new pharmacy system, which will be integrated with the hospital EMR. This is to ensure that when a medication order is placed, the pharmacy system has the information to confirm that the order is for a valid patient.

It means the system will need to know when a patient is registered and when that patient is discharged from the hospital. Or in other words, the pharmacy system will need ADT^A01 (register patient) and ADT^A03 (discharge patient) HL7 messages from the hospital EMR. To put it even more simply, the pharmacy will need A01 and A03 from the hospital EMR.

Acknowledgement Message

Acknowledgement messages are short messages that a receiving system sends back to the sender to confirm that the message was received. This is on top of packet level acknowledgement we discussed earlier. Now we are talking about application level acknowledgement. Whether a complete, fully assembled message was received or not.

Message acknowledgement is very important in HL7. We don't want a situation where messages are getting corrupted or lost on the way and the sending system has no clue. If there was an issue with the message then it's the acknowledgement message that conveys the information back to the sender. This way the sender knows how to fix the issue and resend the message. If there was no acknowledgement at all then that means the message was lost and its time to resend it.

It is important to know that HL7 requires acknowledgement from the application and not just the underlying system. This is to ensure that the message was successfully processed by the receiving application. The Ikea in the HL7 world just doesn't want to know whether you received the parcel, it wants to know whether you were able to assemble the furniture.

There are two kinds of acknowledgement messages in HL7: *original* & *enhanced*. As you can guess, original came before enhanced but the original acknowledgement is nowhere close to being discarded. The original mode of acknowledgement is still the preferred method. It is simple and does the job whereas the enhanced mode has too many bells and whistles and takes a lot more effort to implement.

Original mode is formally known as *Accept Acknowledgement*. Once a message is received by the destination system, it can send back three types of codes. The codes tell you what happened to the original message.

- AA: This is good news. It means the message was successfully processed by the receiving system. It is also commonly referred to as a *positive ack* or just ACK.
- AE: This means the message was processed but there was a problem in the content of the message. This is a *negative ack* or a NAK.
- AR: This means there was a processing error. It could be a wrong message type or some other problem with the receiving system. Maybe the server was down or the database was not available. This error doesn't have anything to do with the content of the message. It too is known as *negative ack* or a NAK.

Enhanced mode is formally known as *Application Acknowledgement*. In this case, there could be up to six different types of codes. Using the Ikea example again, in enhanced mode, Ikea will get two acknowledgements. The first acknowledgement is sent when the parcel is received at the destination, and the second is sent after the furniture is assembled (or not).

The first acknowledgement, confirming that the message was received and safely stored by the receiving system, frees up the sending system from having to wait and see if the message needs to be resent.

The first acknowledgement could generate three types of codes:

- CA: Commit Accept: This means the message was accepted and safely stored by the receiving system.
- CR: Commit Reject: This means the message was rejected and not stored by the receiving system. Maybe the message type was wrong or there was some other problem with the message. An error code is included to provide more information.
- CE: Commit Error: This again means the message was rejected and not stored. In this case the message was rejected because of meta-data issues.

After successful storage, the message is made available to the application and then a second acknowledgement is sent. This acknowledgement is more elaborate where the acknowledgement message structure depends on the message type of the original message and it contains a lot more information than the original mode.

The second acknowledgement message generates the same three error codes, AA, AE and AR that are generated in the original mode. Enhanced mode is like the original mode with an additional acknowledgement for safe storage of message by the receiving system.

6. Message Building Blocks

To the uninitiated, the sight of an HL7 message is often intimidating. A brew of symbols and characters, it looks like something out of the Matrix that is beyond the comprehension of mere mortals. But to be honest, HL7 really is quiet simple and straightforward, once you know how to read it. And for that, you will need to learn about the building blocks of an HL7 message.

Let's take the example of registering a new patient. When the staff at the front desk completes the patient registration and hits enter, it triggers an event: A04 (Register patient). This causes the system to generate a new ADT^A04 HL7 message, which looks something like this.

MSH|^~\&|SENDER_APP|SENT_BY|RECEIVER_APP|RCVD_BY|201310201500
|||ADT^A04|MSG_ID001|P|2.5|||AL

EVN|A04|201310201500||||ID221^Dude@Terminal

PID|1|||PAT416^^^HEALTH_ID||SEBELUS^KANSAS||194801150600|M|||123
SESAME ST^^TORONTO^ON^A1A2B2^CANADA|| (416) 888-8088||ENGLISH
|M|||PAT_AC_721914

NK1|1|SEBELUS^MARY|SPOUSE|||(416) 888-9999|(647) 123 12 34|C|20131020

PV1|1|O|ROOM10^BED12^OUTPATIENT|ELECTIVE||||S21195^DRIKOFF^FR
ANCIS^^^DR^MD||C90023^PAYNE^TRACY^^^DR^MD|SUR||||1|||
S21195^DRIKOFF^FRANCIS^^^DR^MD||37323|SELF|||||||||||||||||||||
||||201310201500

PV2|||DAY SURGERY

AL1|1|FA^PEANUT|||PRODUCES MILD RASH

See what I mean? Makes no sense. But soon it will.

Segment

The primary building block of a message is a *segment*. A segment is simply a row of data in the message. So, for the message above, the first segment starts with MSH and ends on line two with AL. It is actually just one row of data, which was wrapped over to the second line. There is a line break after AL and that means end of the segment. The second segment starts with EVN on line three and ends at "Terminal" on the same line, followed by a line break and so on. A new segment always starts on a new line.

The first three characters of each segment is the segment ID. The segment ID is an acronym or the nametag of the segment.

Once we know the segment name, we know the information in that segment. This is because the main purpose of a segment is to group related information together.

In our example here, there are seven segments (IDs bolded). MSH is the Message Header segment, EVN is the Event segment, PID is the Patient Identification segment and so on. Without even looking at the content of the PID segment, I can tell you it contains the name of the patient, his health ID, date of birth, phone number, address - basically all the information that can be used to identify the patient. Hence the name of the segment - Patient Identification.

MSH I ^~\& I SENDER_APP I SENT_BY I RECEIVER_APP I RCVD_BY I 201310201500 I I ADT^A04 I MSG_ID001 I P I 2.5 I I I AL

EVN I A04 I 201310201500 I I I ID221^Dude@Terminal

PID I 1 I I PAT416^^^HEALTH_ID I I SEBELUS^KANSAS I I 194801150600 I M I I I 123 SESAME ST^^TORONTO^ON^A1A2B2^CANADA I I (416) 888-8088 I I ENGLISH I M I I PAT_AC_721914

NK1 I 1 I SEBELUS^MARY I SPOUSE I I I (416) 888-9999 I (647) 123 12 34 I C I 20131020

PV1 I 1 I O I ROOM10^BED12^OUTPATIENT I ELECTIVE I I I S21195^DRIKOFF^FR ANCIS^^^DR^MD I I C90023^PAYNE^TRACY^^^DR^MD I SUR I I I I 1 I I I S21195^DRIKOFF^FRANCIS^^^DR^MD I I 37323 I SELF I I I I I I I I I I I I I I I I I I I I I I I I 201310201500

PV2 I I I DAY SURGERY

AL1 I 1 I FA^PEANUT I I PRODUCES MILD RASH

Message Structure

Segments in a message are always organized in a specific order. This order is called the message structure. Different message types have different message structures but some things are always the same. For example, every message starts with an MSH segment.

If the order of segments in a message is not exactly like its message structure, then that message will become invalid. It will be rejected by the receiving system.

You can get the abstract message structure of any message in the HL7 specification document. The abstract message structure of an ADT^A04 message is in Chapter 3 of the HL7 specification document where event A04 is discussed.

Here is a partial abstract message structure of an ADT^A04 message. It is just a table with three columns: segment ID, segment name and the chapter where that segment is explained.

Partial Message Structure of ADT^A04

MSH	Message Header	2
[{ SFT }]	Software Segment	2
EVN	Event Type Segment	3
PID	Patient Identification	3
[PD1]	Additional Demographics	3
[{ ROL }]	Role Segment	15
[{ NK1 }]	Next of Kin	3
PV1	Patient Visit Segment	3
[PV2]	Patient Visit – Additional Info.	3
....	....	

If you compare the example message to its abstract message structure, the segment order does not match between the two. In the example message, the SFT segment is missing after MSH; PD1 & ROL are missing too.

Does that mean the example message is invalid? No, it's not because the [ ] and {} brackets around those segments make them either optional or repeatable.

Optional / Repeatable / Mandatory
There are two kinds of brackets: square [ ] and curly {}. If a segment ID is enclosed within [square brackets], it means the segment is optional. We can choose whether to include that segment in the message or not. These segments are generally for

optional information, such as PD1 (additional patient information).

If the segment ID is enclosed within {curly brackets}, then that segment is repeatable. We can have more than one instance of that segment in a real message. Curly brackets are for segments like NK1 (Next of Kin). If a patient has given contact information for two next of kin (spouse and sister), then the information for each next of kin will need a separate NK1 segment in the message.

If a segment ID is enclosed in both [{square and curly}] brackets then that means the segment is both optional and repeatable. If a segment ID is not surrounded by any bracket then that means it is a mandatory segment. That segment has to be present in the message. So segments like MSH, EVN, PID, PV1, with no brackets, have to be present in a real message.

Based on this knowledge we can see why the example is a valid message. All the missing segments, SFT, PD1 and ROL are surrounded by square brackets. And that means those segments are optional. We can choose to leave them out.

Pipe Delimited

So far so good. Now we know that a message is nothing but a collection of segments. Let's dig deeper. Let's take a single segment, for example PID (Patient Identification), and follow the sequence of characters in this segment. You cannot help but notice the | symbol scattered all over the place. This symbol is called a *pipe*.

PID |1| | PAT416^^^HEALTH_ID | | SEBELUS^KANSAS | | 194801150600 | M | | | 123SESAME ST^^TORONTO^ON^A1A2B2^CANADA | | (416) 888-8088 | | ENGLISH | M | | PAT_AC_721914

A pipe is a field separator in HL7. Or, if I were to use the jargon, HL7 messages are pipe delimited.

When you hear delimiter, think separator. Have you ever come across a csv file? Often we convert an excel file into a csv (comma-separated-value) format, to export data. It is a very commonly used file format for updating databases.

When the data in an excel file is converted to csv format, it goes from looking like a table to simple rows of data, like below.

Excel File

Name	Age	Gender
Rick Scott	49	M
Doreen Helner	63	F
Kathy Monderno	81	F

csv File

Name , Age, Gender

Rick Scott, 49, M

Doreen Helner, 63, F

Kathy Monderno, 81, F

Notice how the data has been stripped down to the basics. It is just field values separated by commas. In csv format, a comma is the symbol that separates field values or to use the correct jargon – it is the field delimiter. So now you know what I mean, when I say, a pipe is the field delimiter in HL7. It is the symbol that is used to separate fields in an HL7 message.

Does that mean a segment is just a collection of fields? That's right, a segment is nothing but a collection of related fields. But in HL7, unlike the csv file, there is no top row with the name of individual fields. Then how do we know what those fields represent?

Positional

Fields in a segment are positional. This is another way of saying that the position of a field in the segment is fixed. Patient name is always the fifth field in the PID segment. Date of birth is seventh. You cannot have DOB in the seventh field in one message and in the tenth field in another message. The position of a field is fixed.

The HL7 specification document defines an attribute table for each segment. This attribute table contains the list of fields for each segment and other related information like length of field, data type, etc. Both sending and receiving systems refer to the attribute table to figure out where a particular field is. This eliminates the need to send a header row with field names for each message.

Component (^)

Let's put this newfound knowledge about attribute tables to the test. If you refer to the attribute table for PID segment in Chapter 3 of the HL7 specification document, you will notice that the fifth field is for the name of the patient. Now, we will check the same field in our example message. The best way to get to a field is by counting the pipes.

PID |1 | |PAT416^^^HEALTH_ID | |SEBELUS^KANSAS| |194801150600|M| | |1
23SESAME ST^^TORONTO^ON^A1A2B2^CANADA| |(416) 888-8088| |ENGLISH
|M| |PAT_AC_721914

The value after the fifth pipe is SEBELUS^KANSAS, which does look like a real person's name. You can now claim that you are capable of reading an HL7 message!

However, there is a ^ symbol embedded in the name which needs a little explaining. The ^ symbol is called a *caret*. A caret is the component separator (delimiter) in HL7 messages.

Just like a segment is made up of fields separated by pipes, a field is made up of parts called components, which are separated by carets. If a field has two or more components then those components have to be separated by carets in the message. For example, the name field can have a first name, a middle name, and a last name. So a caret will have to be placed between the first name and the middle name as well as between the middle name and the last name.

Sub-component (&)

Yes, some components are made up of even smaller pieces. Sometimes, I wonder if there were physicists involved in creating HL7. You know, molecules (such as water) are made up of atoms (oxygen and hydrogen). The atoms are made up of sub-atomic particles (electrons, protons & neutrons) and the sub-atomic particles are made up of quarks (up, down, strange, charm etc.).

Similarly, there are components, which are composite in nature and they are made up of smaller pieces called sub-components. Sub-components are separated by the & (ampersand) symbol.

Going back to the example of patient name, its first component, family name, is actually defined as a composite component with five sub-components: surname, own surname prefix, own surname, surname prefix from partner/spouse, and surname from partner/spouse.

If the surname of the patient was St. Pierre Jr. with the first name of Kansas, then the name field would have been something like PIERRE&JR&ST^KANSAS, with subcomponents of the last name separated by & (ampersand).

So there you have it, the building blocks of an HL7 message.

A message is made up of segments
A segment is made up of fields separated by pipes (|)
A field is made up of components separated by a caret (^)
A component is made up of sub-components separated by an ampersand (&)

7. Working with a Message

Now that we have some idea what HL7 is, it's time to start working with complete messages.

What are some of the situations where you are going to be running into an HL7 message?

1. During system integration: If a new clinical system is purchased, it will need to exchange HL7 messages with existing systems.
2. During troubleshooting: If your system is rejecting an incoming message, you will need to look at the error description and the HL7 message.
3. While creating a message profile. If you are a software company then you will need to define what HL7 messages coming out of your system look like.

There could be other situations but these three make it clear that working with HL7 messages involves reading, writing and creating messages.

To read a message, you will need the Interface Specification document (interface spec). It tells you what each field in the message is for. If an interface spec is not available, you can look up the segment attribute table in the HL7 spec to get an idea about the field. However, the source of truth is always the interface spec.

To write a message, you will definitely need an interface spec. This is because an HL7 spec only gives you the abstract framework. Organizations further tweak the rules (for example, only allow numbers in an alphanumeric field) and these rules are documented in the interface spec. To create a valid message, you will need to comply with all the rules.

Creating a message also involves figuring out the information to be included in the message and how it will be mapped. This information is then documented in the interface spec. It takes a while to get all this work done and you will need to know your way around the HL7 spec in order to do so.

But before we get down to reading, writing and creating messages, let's learn a bit more about the HL7 spec and the interface spec so that we are able to navigate them easily.

Anatomy of a Message

I tend to look at an HL7 message as made up of a head and a body. The head is the first two or three segments at the top of the message and the rest is the body. Head segments are *Control* segments and the body segments are *Data* segments.

Control segments only carry meta-data information about a message. Remember Edward Snowden and the NSA spying scandal? At one point, the NSA came back with the excuse that they were only collecting meta-data of phone conversations. In other words, they were not listening to actual conversation, only recording call related information. Things like the duration of the call, the phone number dialed, local time of the call etc.

Similarly, in HL7, control segments carry only meta-data information about a message. Data segments, as the name suggests, are the real carriers of the data.

HL7 Specification Document

There is no escaping it. If you want to know HL7, you will have to know your way around the eminently dry HL7 specification document (HL7 spec). That's where all the information is.

The HL7 spec is the owner's manual for HL7 messaging. It is a bulky manual that has fifteen chapters and over sixteen hundred pages of content.

Until recently, you had to pay a considerable amount to get hold of a copy. However, in September 2012, the organization announced that HL7 standards and all of its intellectual properties would be made publicly available to reduce barriers to adoption and to broaden its usage. You can download the spec for free from their website.

Go to the HL7.org homepage and click on "Standards" in the menu. Within standards, click on "Section 1: Primary Standards" and on the following page (which was a table for me), click on "HL7 Version 2 Product Suite". This will take you to a page that lists all the versions of the standard. I had to register but it was pretty simple (name, email, address). After that, I was able to download a compressed copy of the specification document. The organization still requires that you acquire a license (for free) before using the standard.

Once you unzip the downloaded file, it expands into over twenty different files. This can be a bit overwhelming, like driving in a new city where you don't have a mental layout of the place. To avoid frustration while looking for specific information, it will serve you well to have a good sense of the lay of the land.

ANSI Cover Page.pdf
AppendixA.pdf
AppendixB.pdf
AppendixC.pdf
AppendixD.pdf
CH01.pdf
CH02.pdf
CH02A.pdf
Ch03.pdf
CH04.pdf
CH05.pdf
CH06.pdf
CH07.pdf
CH08.pdf
CH09.pdf
CH10.pdf
CH11.pdf
CH12.pdf
CH13.pdf
CH14.pdf
CH15.pdf
IP Copyright and Trademarks.pdf
Version 2.5 Master Table of Contents.pdf

So, lets unclutter this collection of over twenty files. There are fifteen chapters, four appendices and some other stuff. The chapters are important. You can typically ignore the rest. Even with the chapters, there are only a few that are really important. Remember the 80-20 rule?

Chapter 2 (CH02.pdf) is the most important chapter in the collection. This chapter is called "Control" and that is where you will find information on all the important concepts, control segments, fields, data types etc.

HL7 also defines a lot of data types, which are in CH02A.pdf. You can ignore this chapter unless you need details of a particular data type.

Then there are Chapters 3–15. Each chapter handles a different message type, its trigger events, its data types and other related details.

Each chapter has more or less the same layout. First, trigger events and message types are discussed. Then some data segments are introduced, followed by examples and finally special scenarios.

Interface Specification Document

I mentioned earlier that the HL7 spec is like the owner's manual. This statement needs a correction. The real owners' manual is the Interface Specification Document (interface spec). HL7 spec is more like a rulebook with multiple options. The interface spec is a customized version of that rulebook.

Interface specs vary depending on the type of interfaces we are talking about. If it is only for sending and receiving messages, then the spec will detail what the message will look like going out and what it should look like coming in, before the system will process it.

For integration engines (hubs), the spec looks different. They receive a message, change the type/content of the message and send out a different message. So in addition to sending and receiving messages, the interface spec will also have to provide details on transforming the message.

There is no set structure for an interface spec. People do their own thing. But there are some common pieces of information they all have.

The spec will define one or more trigger events. It could even define an entire message type with all of its trigger events.

Generally, you will have a number of different specs for different trigger events and message types.

Within the spec, for each trigger event, you will have a message structure that defines the segments and their order in the message. And for each segment, there will be an attribute table, which defines the length, optionality, data type, and other details for each field of that segment. Message structure and segment details give you pretty much all the information you will need to read and write messages.

Reading/Writing a Message

Here is the example message from the previous chapter. Let's take a stab at reading it.

```
MSH|^~\&|SENDER_APP|SENT_BY|RECEIVER_APP|RCVD_BY|201310201500
||ADT^A04|MSG_ID001|P|2.5|||AL

EVN|A04|201310201500||||ID221^Dude@Terminal

PID|1|||PAT416^^^HEALTH_ID||SEBELUS^KANSAS||194801150600|M|||123
SESAME ST^^TORONTO^ON^A1A2B2^CANADA|| (416) 888-8088||ENGLISH
|M||PAT_AC_721914

NK1|1|SEBELUS^MARY|SPOUSE|||(416) 888-9999|(647) 123 12 34|C|20131020

PV1|1|O|ROOM10^BED12^OUTPATIENT|ELECTIVE|||S21195^DRIKOFF^FRA
NCIS^^^DR^MD||C90023^PAYNE^TRACY^^^DR^MD|SUR|||||1|||
S21195^DRIKOFF^FRANCIS^^^DR^MD||37323|SELF||||||||||||||||||||||||
||||201310201500

PV2|||DAY SURGERY

AL1|1|FA^PEANUT||PRODUCES MILD RASH
```

First thing you look for in a message is its message type and trigger event. Message type is the ninth field in the MSH segment (MSH-9). In our case, its value is ADT^A04 (bolded in the message). Remember, this is a field with two components joined together by a component delimiter (^). The first component is the general message type, which is ADT. This means the message has something to do with patient administration. The second component is the event type code. This is the trigger event that generated the message. In our example it is A04, which means a patient registration triggered this message.

When you are working with messages, you will be regularly checking their trigger event codes. MSH-9 is one place to check but there is another field that holds the trigger event code. It is the first field of the EVN segment (EVN-1). I personally prefer this field because it is easier to locate in a message. Just look for EVN segment and right after it you have the trigger event code. You can confirm this in the example message. The code is the same in both the fields - A04.

Once you know the trigger event code, you know the information in the message. For example, since A04 is the trigger event code for patient registration, it implies the message contains information about a patient registration.

Whenever you are reading an HL7 message, you are looking for specific information. No matter what information you are looking for, you will need to know the field in the message body where that information is. For that, you turn to the interface spec and look for the field that holds that information.

Let's take an example. Suppose you want to find out the patient who was registered at the hospital on October 20, 2013 at 3:00 PM. Your technical guys have narrowed down the search to a single message, the example message above, and now you want to confirm that this is the message that has the patient's name.

For that, you will first need to locate the field for date and time of registration and confirm that it is October 20, 2013 3:00 PM. After confirming it, you will look for the name of the patient.

So where could be the date and time of registration in the message? Date and time – that sounds like meta-data. Let's look in the control segments.

There are two control segments in our example message - MSH & EVN. If you consult their attribute tables in the spec (HL7 or interface), you will notice that neither has a field for date and time of registration. Welcome to the world of HL7! Dealing with ambiguity is a prerequisite.

We do have a couple of other date/time fields. MSH-7 (Date/Time of Message) holds date/time for when the message was generated and EVN-2 (Recorded Date/Time) holds the date/time for when the trigger event was fired. Generally, as in our example, these fields have the same value. But if there is a difference, then I'll go with EVN-2. It sounds more like the date and time of patient's registration.

The value in EVN-2 is 201310201500. To interpret this, we again check the EVN attribute table and look for the data format of EVN-2. The format is YYYYMMDDHHMM, where Y is the year, M is the month, and so on. After parsing the content we get the year as 2013, the month as 10 (October), the day as 20 and the time as 1500 or 3PM. This is the message we are looking for.

Ok, we have our message. Now, on to the second part – finding the patient's name. Patient's name is without doubt clinical data. It has to be in a data segment. There are five data segments in the message and that is where we will search for the patient's name. The data segments are:

PID – Patient Identification Segment

NK1 – Next of Kin Segment

PV1 – Patient Visit Segment

PV2 – Patient Visit – Additional Info. Segment &

AL1 – Allergy Information Segment

It is not hard to guess just by looking at the names of the segments that patient's name field probably is in the PID segment. Of course, there could be a situation where things are not as obvious (like the date/time field earlier). In that case we will have to search the interface spec for that field. It does get boring sometimes.

To confirm our hunch we check the attribute table of the PID segment and sure enough the 5th field (PID-5) is the name of the patient. In the message, we count five pipes and the value after the fifth pipe, SEBELUS^KANSAS, is the patient's name. We have successfully read the message and found that Kansas Sebelus was the patient who was registered at the hospital on October 20, 2013 at 3:00 PM.

Writing a message is just the reverse of reading it. In the case of writing, you refer to the interface spec and build the message by populating fields with appropriate values. Patient name goes in PID-5, date of birth goes in PID-7 and so on.

Creating a Message

Now it's time to create a message or to be precise, a message profile, where you define its exact structure. This is involved work and usually a business or interface analyst will be doing it full time.

To create a message, you again start with the trigger event. If you are creating the profile for patient registration, you start with A04.

A04, like every other trigger event, has its abstract message structure defined in the HL7 spec. The first task is to create a bare bones message structure by eliminating all the optional segments. A message structure made up of only the required segments, like below.

MSH
EVN
PID
PV1

This, then, is the simplest message structure of an A04 message.

Next, depending on additional information that has to be sent, you include other optional segments from the abstract message structure, at appropriate places within the bare bones message structure.

The example message has three optional segments - information on family members (NK1), additional information about the visit (PV2) and allergy information (AL1). Inclusion of these segments at their appropriate locations changes the message structure.

MSH

EVN

PID

[{NK1}]

PV1

[PV2]

[{AL1}]

This then is the message structure of the example A04 message. After the message structure is defined, you customize the attribute table for each segment and the job is done. Another message has been defined. Others can read this information in the interface spec and they will know what an A04 message coming out of your system will look like.

Segment Attribute Table

We have talked a lot about the segment attribute table, so let's take a moment to learn more about it. A segment attribute table contains the list of fields in a segment. It also includes other details such as which fields are optional, which can repeat, etc. All segment attribute tables in the interface spec are derived from the abstract tables in the HL7 spec.

To customize a segment attribute table, the basic rule is that you can only constrain. You can add more conditions and rules but you cannot remove existing rules defined by HL7.

What conditions can you add? Look at the columns in the segment attribute table below. Let's use LEN (length) as an example. The table defines 250 characters as the length of the patient name field (5th field). You can reduce the field length to 50 characters. No problem. What you cannot do is increase field length to 300 characters. That will violate the rule of 250 character limit set by HL7.

Attribute Table – PID – Patient Identification

SEQ	LEN	DT	OPT	RP#	TBL#	ITEM#	ELEMENT NAME
1	4	SI	O			00104	Set ID - PID
2	20	CX	B			00105	Patient ID
3	250	CX	R	Y		00106	Patient Identifier List
4	20	CX	B	Y		00107	Alternate Patient ID - PID
5	250	XPN	R	Y		00108	Patient Name
6	250	XPN	O	Y		00109	Mother's Maiden Name
7	26	TS	O			00110	Date/Time of Birth
8	1	IS	O		0001	00111	Administrative Sex
...	...	...	...	...	...	...	

Source: HL7 Specification Document v2.5, Chapter 3

And, as you can see, the column headings of the segment attribute table are not exactly intuitive. So here is a description of what they stand for.

SEQ: *Sequence Number.* This is just the position of the field in the segment. Set ID is the first field in the PID segment, Date of Birth is the seventh field, Sex is the eighth and so on.

LEN: *Maximum Length of the Field.* Nothing to explain here.

DT: *Data Type.* HL7 likes to control how the data is represented in the message and it does so through data types. This column defines the data type of the field.

OPT: *Optionality.* This column tells you whether you are required to have a value in the field or if it is optional. A field can be Required (R), Optional (O) or Conditional (C). If it is conditional, it means the optionality is based on another field. For example, Blood Type is a conditional field. It is optional normally but if the patient is admitted for surgery then it becomes a required field.

Another letter (B) can also be seen in this column. It is for backward compatibility. These fields are present only to support older versions of HL7. Unless you are supporting that version, you should leave those fields empty.

RP #: *Repetition (number).* This column tells you if the field can repeat. If the field is blank or has an "N" then no repetition of the field is allowed. If the field has a "Y" then it can repeat one or more times. If it has a number, such as Y(3), then that field can repeat up to 3 times. Field repetition values are separated by a ~ (tilde) in the message.

TBL #: *Table Number.* For some fields, HL7 only allows a specific set of values. For example, in the *Administrative Sex* field, only the first letter of patient's gender (M, F, U) is allowed. You cannot put "Male" in this field. These valid values are defined in a table with a unique table number. If a field takes its values from a table then that table number is listed in this column, as is the case with the sex field.

ITEM #: *ID Number.* This is a number that uniquely identifies every field in the HL7 specification document. Field "Date/Time of Birth" is at the seventh field position in the PID segment and its ID is 00110. The same field is at the sixteenth position in the segment NK1 but the ID is the same, 00110. Keep in mind the subtle difference in field names though. "Name" and "Patient Name" are different fields and they have different ID's.

ELEMENT NAME: *Name of the Field.* This is just a descriptive name of the field.

8. Control Segments

From the last chapter, if you remember the discussion about the anatomy of a message, control segments are the segments in the head of a message. They only carry meta-data information about a message.

There are about a dozen control segments defined by HL7. They are all explained in chapter 2 of the HL7 spec. Fortunately, we only need to know about a few of them to account for the vast majority of cases. For example, there are control segments for breaking a very large message into smaller pieces and control segments for batching together a large number of messages. These control segments are not used that frequently and for a general understanding, you can skip them.

There are five control segments that you really should know about – MSH, EVN, NTE, MSA & ERR. We will start with MSH, the ubiquitous control segment that every message begins with. It is the most important control segment. If you decide five is too many for your precious time and you are only going to read about one, then let this be the one.

Message Header Segment (MSH)

The message header segment (MSH) is the most important control segment. Every HL7 message starts with this segment. When an HL7 message is received by a system, it is the MSH that tells the receiving system where this message came from, the information it contains and how it is supposed to be acknowledged.

This is a segment you want to know well.

To get a better understanding of the contents of this segment, let's use the MSH segment from our example A04 message and explore its contents.

MSH | ^~\& | SENDER_APP | SENT_BY | RECEIVER_APP | RCVD_BY | 201310201500
| | ADT^A04 | MSG_ID001 | P | 2.5 | | | AL

If you break the segment down into its separate fields, it gets easier to figure out the content. Remember | is used to separate fields.

MSH | ^~\& | SENDER_APP | SENT_BY | RECEIVER_APP | RCVD_BY

MSH-1: |
MSH-2: ^~\&
MSH-3: SENDER_APP
MSH-4: SENT_BY
MSH-5: RECEIVER_APP
MSH-6: RCVD_BY

201310201500 | | ADT^A04 | MSG_ID001 | P | 2.5 | | | AL

MSH-7: 201310201500
MSH-8:
MSH-9: ADT^A04
MSH-10: MSG_ID001
MSH-11: P
MSH-12: 2.5
MSH-13:
MSH-14:
MSH-15: AL

Note that some of the fields are empty (e.g. MSH-8). This is perfectly fine. Remember, not every field in a segment is required to have a value. If you refer to the segment attribute table of MSH, you can confirm that all missing fields are optional.

Now, here is a little insider information. There are only a few fields in each segment that are really important and regularly used. That is why you see the usual pipe pattern (| | | |) in HL7 messages. The consecutive pipes are nothing but empty fields.

So keeping with our tradition, and saving you precious time, we are going to discuss only the most important fields in a segment.

In the MSH segment, owing to the fact that it contains most of the meta-data information, there are many important fields. It is the heaviest control segment. Some of these important fields are required and others are optional, but they almost always have a value.

If you refer to the segment attribute table of the MSH segment, HL7 requires that the following fields always have a value.

MSH-1:   Field Separator
MSH-2:   Encoding Characters
MSH-7:   Date/Time Of Message
MSH-9:   Message Type
MSH-10:   Message Control ID
MSH-11:   Processing ID
MSH-12:   Version ID

It is easy to find out which fields are required in a segment. Just go to the segment attribute table and look for the letter R in the optionality (OPT) column.

Besides these required fields, there are some other fields (below) in MSH, which are optional but regularly used. They are important and I think you should know about them.

MSH-3:   Sending Application
MSH-4:   Sending Facility
MSH-5:   Receiving Application
MSH-6:   Receiving Facility
MSH-15:   Accept Acknowledgement Type
MSH-16:   Application Acknowledgement Type

Keep in mind though that this is only my personal opinion. Others can argue that there are other optional fields that are important and some here are not. I'm not denying it. But from my experience, I believe these are the important fields in the MSH segment.

Now let's get familiar with these fields because the name of the field doesn't tell you even one tenth of the story.

MSH-1: Field Separator

Usually, the first field in a segment is the field that follows the segment ID. So technically "encoding characters" should be the first field of MSH segment. But with MSH, there is an anomaly. The first field (MSH-1) always defines the symbol that will be the field separator (delimiter) for the entire message. If you remember the discussion about pipe delimiters in Chapter 6, | is the field separator in HL7 messages and therefore, the first field of MSH. But it doesn't have to be. You can choose to have a comma (,) or any other symbol as the separator. If you choose to use a comma, the segment will look something like this.

```
MSH,^~\&,SENDER_APP,SENT_BY,RECEIVER_APP,RCVD_BY,201310201500,,AD
T^A04,MSG_ID001,P,2.5,,,AL
```

This would be a perfectly legitimate HL7 segment. However, | has become such a de facto standard that no one really uses anything but | as the field delimiter. But it's good to know that we have the power to change it.

MSH-2: Encoding Characters

Encoding Characters are the four symbols ^ ~ \ & that HL7 reserves for message construction.

These characters have special meaning, which allows applications reading an HL7 message to distinguish between components and subcomponents of a field, read repeating fields, and translate symbols.

The encoding characters, in order, are - Component Separator (^), Repetition Separator (~), Escape Character (\) and Sub Component Separator (&). The position of each character is fixed in the field. First the component separator then the repetition separator and so on.

By having these symbols in MSH-2, we are basically saying that in this HL7 message, ^ will be used to separate components, ~ will be used to separate multiple occurrences of a field, \ will be used for special characters and & will be used to separate sub components.

But shouldn't this be hardcoded in systems that read HL7 messages, instead of including it in every message?

Good point. The reason encoding characters are included in every HL7 message is because these characters are customizable too, just like the field separator | .

HL7 gives you the option of selecting your own encoding characters. If you don't like ^ and would rather have # as the component separator in your messages then all you have to do is replace ^ with # in MSH-2. As a result, your encoding characters would be #~\&. The # symbol will now be the component separator.

But this whole discussion is pointless! Over the years, these symbols have become a de facto standard. I'll bet, many folks who have been working with HL7 for years, don't know that you can change these symbols. I have never come across a message where a different set of symbols were used.

Before we move to the next field, you need to know more about the other two encoding characters – the Repetition Separator (~) and the Escape Character (\).

Repetition Separator (~): This is the symbol that separates multiple values in a field. Remember the section on segment attribute table in chapter 7? Some fields are repeatable and they can have multiple values. ~ is the symbol that is used to separate those values in a field.

In the MSH segment, field MSH-18 and field MSH-21 are repeatable. This means, whenever those fields have two or more values, the values will be separated by the ~ symbol. If a system reading the message comes across the ~ symbol, it will know right away that what follows is the next value of the field.

Escape Character (\): HL7 reserves encoding characters for message construction and they have a special meaning in the message. What happens if you need to use one of those special characters as part of the data? The application reading the message is going to be all confused!!

In real world applications, the most troublesome of these special characters is the ampersand symbol (&). It is used for "and" (as in Ben & Jerry's) and is also a commonly used symbol in programming languages like HTML (which could be embedded in an HL7 message). So, sooner or later, you are bound to come across the & symbol in the body of an HL7 message.

What happens if these characters are part of the data? Let's consider an example.

Ben & Jerry's Diagnostic Center sends the result of a test as an HL7 message to the ordering hospital. The hospital system receives the message and starts reading it to parse the data (pull out field values) and save it to a database. When the system gets to the Sending Facility field (MSH-4), it will read "Ben" and then run into the & symbol. At that point, the system is being told that the name of the facility has a sub-component. Facility names don't have sub-components (if you check the segment attribute table), so in all likelihood the system doesn't have a corresponding field in the database to save the value "Jerry's Diagnostic Center".

This is a recipe for application failure. Let's assume this is a futuristic, can-handle-anything kind of system, but even then the system is only saving "Ben" as the name of the sending facility, which is incorrect. The doctor reading the lab report will see that "Ben" sent the test result. I don't know how much faith she will have in the report.

So what do we do? We can't ask Ben & Jerry's Diagnostic Center to change its name.

This is where the escape character comes to the rescue. If characters, which have special meaning in HL7, need to be transmitted as part of the data, then all one needs to do is replace the character with its corresponding escape sequence. The system reading it will read the escape sequence and replace it with that special character before saving it.

An escape sequence is nothing more than one or more characters surrounded by the escape character (\). Every special character in HL7 has a corresponding escape sequence. There are many escape sequences for formatting and highlighting text, and you can even create custom escape sequences.

Here are the escape sequences for the symbols we have already discussed:

Escape Sequences

Use	Special Character	Escape Sequence
Field Separator	|	\F\
Component Separator	^	\S\
Sub-Component Separator	&	\T\
Repetition Separator	~	\R\
Escape Character	\	\E\

Source: HL7 Specification Document v2.5, Chapter 2

Guess how Ben & Jerry's Diagnostic Center will be encoded in an HL7 message. You will replace the encoding character & with its corresponding escape sequence so that you will have "Ben \T\ Jerry's Diagnostic Center" encoded in the message. The receiving system will recognize \T\ as an escape sequence and replace it with the & symbol when the data is saved locally.

MSH-3: Sending Application & MSH-4: Sending Facility

Fields three and four are optional, but they are almost always populated in real world implementations. They contain the name of the application and the facility that sent the message (the sending system). Often these fields are used as filter to process or route messages based on the sending application and facility.

For an example, if Ben & Jerry's Diagnostic Center is running a Meditech system, then the sending application will be "Meditech" in MSH-3 and the sending facility, "Ben & Jerry's Diagnostic Center" (or an abbreviation B&J DIAG) will be in the MSH-4 field.

MSH-5: Receiving Application & MSH-6: Receiving Facility

Fields five and six are similar to fields three and four except that they contain the name of the application and the facility that the message is being sent to (the receiver). These fields too are used in real world implementations as a filter to route or process messages based on the intended recipient.

MSH-7: Date/Time of Message

This is a required field. It captures the date and time when the sending system created the message. In a North American context, the field is usually populated in the format YYYYMMDDHHMM (where Y = year, M = month and so on). Some sites go to a higher degree of precision and include seconds or even milliseconds in the field. HL7 allows up to 26 characters, so we have a lot of room here!

MSH-9: Message Type

Message Type is a very important field and a valid value in this field is required for every message. This is the field that tells the receiving system the type of message it is. Knowing the type of message is essential for a system to be able to read the message.

Without this information, the receiving system will be like the early archeologists in Egypt. They had no idea what the birds and the eyes in hieroglyphs meant. It wasn't until the Rosetta stone was discovered by Napoleon's troops and Champollion figured out a way to read it, that hieroglyphs started to make sense. This is what message type does to the receiving system.

The message type field has three components – Message Type (MSH-9.1), Trigger Event (MSH-9.2) and Message Structure ID (MSH-9.3). In our example, this field has the value ADT^A04. Notice something? Only the first two components are there. This is fine because the third component is an optional component and usually we leave it empty. If you want to know the Message Structure ID of a message, you can look it up in HL7 specs where the abstract message structure is defined. It's in the heading.

We have already discussed message types (MSH-9.1) and trigger events (MSH-9.2). If you need to refresh, they are in Chapter 5.

MSH-10: Message Control ID

The purpose of this field is to uniquely identify each and every message. Usually, the value in this field is a unique number generated by the sending system. For each subsequent message, the sending system increments this number by one to generate another unique number. Some systems also attach a date stamp at the end of the number to eliminate any chances of duplication.

Why do we need to uniquely identify each message?

When the receiving system gets the message, it has to send an acknowledgement back to the sending system. Acknowledgement tells the sending system if the message was received ok and if it can move on or whether there are defects in the message and it needs to resend it. The receiving system uses the Message Control ID to tell the sending system which message it is talking about. And that is why we need to uniquely identify each and every message.

Troubleshooting is another reason why we need a unique ID for every message. At the time of debugging and testing, MSH-10 is an invaluable piece of information. It helps track down an individual message in a haystack of messages.

MSH-11: Processing ID

This is a required field, which contains a single character. It signals whether the message is real (production in techie speak) or just for testing. If the value is P, it signals that it is a production or real message. If the value is T (Test/ Training) or D (Development) then it is a test message.

MSH-12: Version ID

This is another required field that is of interest only to developers and interface analysts. This field contains the version number of HL7 that the message conforms to. In our example this value is 2.5, which means the message conforms to HL7 version 2.5.

MSH-15: Accept Acknowledgement Type & MSH-16: Application Acknowledgement Type

Remember the discussion on message acknowledgement in chapter 5? Even if you do, here's a quick recap.

There are two types of acknowledgement messages – original & enhanced. In the original mode only one acknowledgement message is sent. It is sent by the receiving application, hence its name, application acknowledgement.

In the enhanced mode, two acknowledgement messages are sent. One is the application acknowledgement and the other one is accept acknowledgement. Accept acknowledgement is sent when the receiving system has successfully saved the message at its end.

In other words, in enhanced mode, when the receiving system accepts the delivered message, it sends out an accept acknowledgement. It then sends the message to the application, which does its own verification and sends out an application acknowledgement.

Fields MSH-15 and MSH-16 act like switches for these two acknowledgement types. If the value is AL in MSH-15 then the receiving system is supposed to "ALways" send an accept acknowledgement. If the value is NE then it should "NEver"

84

send an accept acknowledgement. The same codes are used in the MSH-16 field, only this time it pertains to the application acknowledgement message.

For most practical purposes, these fields are useless. This is because we don't use enhanced mode of acknowledgement much. Usually people just leave these fields empty, which means original mode. If you want to use the enhanced mode, then you will have to have AL in both the fields. If you just want to know that the message was received successfully, then you will have AL in MSH-15 as in our example message.

Event Type Segment (EVN)

Event Type is a required control segment in many message types, such as patient administration (ADT) and financial management (BAR). It is a short segment with seven fields, only one of which is required. It has "good to know" kind of information but nothing critical. But the segment is so common in HL7 messages that I felt you should know about it.

The only useful information this segment has, in my opinion, is the time when the event happened, EVN-2.

Here is the EVN segment from the example message.

EVN | A04 | 201310201500 | | | ID221^Dude@Terminal

EVN-1: A04   - Event Type Code
EVN -2: 201310201500   - Recorded Date/Time
EVN -3:
EVN-4:
EVN-5: ID221^Dude@Terminal   - Operator ID
EVN-6:
EVN-7:

This example is very typical of EVN segments in the real world. You have the trigger event code (A04) in the first field even though it is not required and is a repeat from MSH-9.2. And then there is the Recorded Date/Time, the only required field in this segment. Among the optional fields, EVN-1 and EVN-5 are generally populated.

EVN-1: Event Type Code

As the name suggests, this field holds the trigger event code. It is a duplicate of MSH-9.2 and retained for use by systems using older versions of HL7.

You will always find this field populated. This is because EVN-1 used to hold the trigger event code before a newer version of HL7 came along and moved the trigger event code to MSH-9.2. People kept populating the value in EVN-1 to maintain compatibility with older versions. Who wanted to come back and recode the interfaces! A little duplication didn't sound like a big price to pay and now it's baked in.

EVN-2: Recorded Date/Time

This is the only required field in this segment. It holds the date and time (YYYYMMDDHHMMSS) of the trigger event. To use our example message, the value in EVN-2 is the moment when, after filling out the form, the person at the desk hits the submit button to register the patient.

EVN-5: Operator ID

This is an optional field that holds the identifying information of the person at the desk. It identifies the "dude" at the terminal. He is the one who hit the submit button to register the patient. The field contains his employee ID and name.

Now you know where to look if you want to find out who did the registration.

Notes & Comments Segment (NTE)

NTE is a general purpose segment. As the name suggests, this is a segment for notes and comments. You will find this segment peppered all over the place in order and report messages.

If you look at the abstract message structure of a general order (ORM^O01) or a result (ORU^R01) message, you will find NTE at multiple places. And it is always enclosed between square and curly brackets; it's always optional and repeatable.

The reason this segment is in multiple places is because an NTE is always associated with the segment it came after. If an NTE is after a PID segment, it holds notes & comments about the patient. If it is after OBX segment (result) then it holds notes & comments about the result.

The segment itself is very short. It only has four fields, which are all optional.

NTE-1: Set ID - NTE

This field assigns a number to an NTE segment. NTE commonly repeats to accommodate long comments and this field helps to identify individual segments in that comment.

Numbering starts at 1 and increases by increments of one until that comment is done. The next time another NTE is used, the numbering starts again from 1. So if there is a comment about the patient, it will have a bunch of NTEs numbered 1 to n. If there is another group of NTEs for result, they too will be numbered 1 to n.

I have come across messages with beautifully formatted comments and dotted borders. They really grab your attention in a sea of random characters. Who says techies aren't artistic!

Let's consider an example. Suppose the following comments were to be included in an order message for a blood test:

Patient comment (after PID)
The patient was very particular about his breakfast. He consumed an orange before the blood was drawn.

Order comment (after OBR)

If the test results will be affected because of consumption of a citrus fruit, please give us a call. We will cancel this order and create another one.

A creative sender with a flair for design could send the comments something like this:

```
PID | .......
NTE | 1 | | --------------------------------------------------------------------- |
NTE | 2 | | The patient was very particular about his breakfast |
NTE | 3 | | He consumed an orange before the blood was drawn |
NTE | 4 | | --------------------------------------------------------------------- |
.
.
OBR | .....
NTE | 1 | | ---------------------------------------------------------------------- |
NTE | 2 | If the test results will be affected because of consumption |
NTE | 3 | of a citrus fruit, please give us a call |
NTE | 4 | | We will cancel this order and create another one |
NTE | 5 | | ---------------------------------------------------------------------- |
```

Notice how the NTE segments are numbered 1,2,3,4… for each comment. That is the Set ID to identify individual NTE's in a group.

NTE-3: Comment

This is the field that holds the actual notes & comments in free-form text. You can even format the text (highlight etc.) by including appropriate escape sequences.

Acknowledgement Control Segments

A general acknowledgement message is made entirely of control segments. Of course, MSH is the first segment in the message. It is always the first segment, no matter what the message type. After that you have MSA, the acknowledgement segment and if there are errors, you will have ERR segments. That's it. These are the only segments in an acknowledgement message.

HL7 does allow customized acknowledgement messages but in real life, we only use the general acknowledgement message with its simple message structure.

For a successful message, a positive acknowledgement (ACK in short form) is sent, which is even simpler and has only two types of segments - MSH & MSA. For example,

```
MSH I ^~\ & I RECEIVER_APP I RCVD_BY I SENDER_APP I SENT_BY I 201310201501
I I ADT^A04 I R_MSG_ID279 I P I 2.5 I I I AL
MSA I AA I MSG_ID001 I Got your message
```

For an unsuccessful message, a negative acknowledgement (NAK in short form) is sent, which can have three types of segments (MSH, MSA & ERR). The ERR segment can repeat if there is more than one error to report.

In the example below we have two errors to report, hence two ERR segments.

```
MSH I ^~\ & I RECEIVER_APP I RCVD_BY I SENDER_APP I SENT_BY I 201310201501
I I ADT^A04 I R_MSG_ID279 I P I 2.5 I I I AL
MSA I AE I MSG_ID001 I Can't read this message.
ERR I I PID^5 I 101^Required field missing I E
ERR I I PID^7 I 102^Data type error I E
```

Now, let's look more closely at these control segments (MSA & ERR) in an acknowledgement message.

Message Acknowledgement Segment (MSA)

MSA is a required segment in every acknowledgement message. This is the segment that holds the acknowledgement code, which tells you if the receiver was able to process the message or not.

The segment has six fields, out of which only the first two are required. In practice, the third field, which is optional, is also populated. The last three are always empty.

MSA-1: Acknowledgement Code

When people look at acknowledgement messages, this is the first field their eyes go to. The first field of the MSA segment holds the all-important acknowledgement code.

The acknowledgement code is made up of two uppercase letters. If the value is AA that means all is good. For error messages, we have two codes – AE and AR.

AE means there is a problem with the message. It could be its content, structure or something else but most probably the source of the problem is the sender. If it is AR, then that means there is some other system level problem, such as disk space issues or a power failure. In this case, the source of the problem could be the receiver and most probably you will need to resend the message.

MSA-2: Message Control ID

This is the second required field in the MSA segment. It contains the Message Control ID (MSH-10) of the original message. If you remember, the message control ID uniquely identifies a message and by including it here, the acknowledgement message is indicating that this acknowledgement is for the message with control ID in MSA-2.

Let's clarify this with the help of an example below. The original message has its control ID in MSH-10 (MSG_ID001) and the same control ID is in MSA-2 of the acknowledgement message. Keep in mind though, that the acknowledgement message also has its message control ID in MSH-10 (R_MSG_ID279), which is different from the message control ID of the original message.

(Original Message)
MSH I ^~\ & I SENDER_APP I SENT_BY I RECEIVER_APP I RCVD_BY I 201310201500 I I ADT^A04 I **MSG_ID001** I P I 2.5 I I I AL

(Acknowledgement Message)
MSH I ^~\ & I RECEIVER_APP I RCVD_BY I SENDER_APP I SENT_BY I 201310201501 I I ADT^A04 I R_MSG_ID279 I P I 2.5 I I I AL
MSA I AA I **MSG_ID001** I Got your message

Without this ID, there is no way for the sending system to know which message the receiver is acknowledging.

MSA-3: Text Message

This is an optional field that can be used to send additional information like error details. Newer versions of HL7 don't recommend using this field. We have a brand new segment (ERR) to provide detailed information about errors.

Error Segment (ERR)

The ERR segment is included in an acknowledgement message when there is an error to report. This segment is used to provide more details about the error condition.

For each error condition, a separate ERR segment is created. In the example, we have two ERR segments, which implies there were two issues in the message.

```
ERR | | PID^5 | 101^Required field missing | E
ERR | | PID^7 | 102^Data type error | E
```

There are twelve fields in this segment. Two are required and the rest are optional.

ERR-2: Error Location

This is an optional field but it almost always has a value. It identifies the segment and field where the error happened.

In our example, for the two ERR segments, the values are PID-5 and PID-7. This means there was a problem with the "Patient Name" (PID-5) field and the "Patient Date of Birth" (PID-7) field. It looks like we are missing the patient name and the date of birth was sent in the wrong format.

ERR-3: HL7 Error Code

This is a required field that contains a three-digit error code. HL7 defines a table of general error conditions (in HL7 spec) with a code number for each condition. The value in our example is from that table. For example, if a required field is missing in the message, then the value in ERR-3 is 101.

This is another required field, which contains a single character, for the "error severity" code. There are only three values for this field, I (Information), W (Warning) and E (Error). Usually, if we are sending error information, it is because there was an error. No one bothers with information and warning messages. The value here is almost always E.

9. Data Segments

Now we come to the meat and potatoes of HL7 messaging. Data segments form the body of an HL7 message. They carry patient and clinical data, the thing that matters the most. Rest of the message is just the box, styrofoam packaging and the shipping label.

The main purpose of a data segment is to group together similar data in one place. For example, all the information about a patient is grouped together in a segment called PID (Patient Identification segment). Actually, there are so many data fields about the patient that there is one more segment, PD1, for additional patient data.

Similarly, all patient visit information is in PV1, allergy info is in AL1, insurance information is in IN1 and so on. Each segment is described in detail in the HL7 spec.

There is another kind of data segment that you will occasionally come across in a message. These are locally defined segments or what we call Z segments. HL7 allows users to define their own segment if they want to send additional information for which there is no field defined by HL7. Unfortunately, this is a much abused privilege. I have come across messages where you have the bare minimum mandatory segments, followed by rows of Z segments with the actual data.

In this chapter, we will look at some of the most commonly used data segments.

There are close to 150 data segments defined in the HL7 spec. Not even the experts are expected to know about all of them. It is always a good idea to keep the HL7 specs handy so whenever the need arises, you can quickly look up a particular segment and its details.

For a general understanding, you only need to know about a few of these data segments. The 80-20 rule applies to data segments too. Only about twenty percent of data segments are actually used in eighty percent of messages. So for a busy professional like you, it makes sense to invest the limited time you have, in that twenty percent.

There are three message types that account for most of that twenty percent.
- ADT (Patient Administration – Chapter 3)
- ORM (Order Entry – Chapter 4)
- ORU (Observation Reporting – Chapter 7)

If you get a good handle on these, I'm sure you can handle any exotic message that gets thrown at you. The HL7 spec is your friend and don't forget to ask the vendor for their interface spec. Between these two documents, you can figure out almost any HL7 message.

ADT (Patient Administration)

Patient Administration messages are at the heart of HL7 messaging. I am not sure how they came to be known as ADT messages, probably it is a reference to three commonly occurring trigger events – Admit, Discharge & Transfer.

This message type is all about the patient. Its primary use is to make sure various systems in a healthcare organization are in sync with patient info, such as the patient status in the hospital, contact info, medication, allergies, etc.

In a typical healthcare organization, there is usually an EMR or a registration system that manages patient records and updates other ancillary clinical systems through HL7 ADT messages. It is through these messages that a patient's status and information is kept synchronized across the organization and beyond.

From the moment a person starts interacting with the hospital, HL7 messages start getting generated in response to real world events (trigger events). This is how other systems always have the latest information about a patient.

Let's consider an example. A person walks into the outpatient unit of a hospital. The first thing that happens is patient registration at the front desk. This real world event is a trigger event, Event A04 (Register a Patient). When it happens, the system automatically generates an ADT^A04 message to let other systems know that a new patient has been registered with the hospital.

Let's say all is not looking well for the patient and the doctor decides to keep him in the hospital for observation. This means the person is getting admitted to the hospital. This is another trigger event, Event A01 (Admit/Visit Notification). This event will cause another HL7 message, ADT^A01, to be generated. If the patient is getting admitted to the hospital, it means he will need a bed, a nurse will be assigned for care and medication will have to be ordered. All the ancillary systems, nursing, bed management, pharmacy, finance, food services etc. will receive the ADT^A01 message, so that they know about this new patient and any necessary follow-up action can be taken by them.

The next day, the patient is doing much better and the doctor says he is free to go home. He is given his medication, someone arrives to take him home and he is discharged by the administration system. This is another trigger event, Event A03 (Discharge/End Visit). This trigger event generates an HL7 message, ADT^A03, so that other systems can update their records and close the patient account. We don't want a situation where someone is ordering controlled drugs from pharmacy on behalf of a patient who has already been discharged!

This was a simple example. In real life, between registration and discharge, a patient's record can undergo a lot of changes. The doctor could change, the patient could get transferred to another unit/bed or the patient's contact could change. All these changes have corresponding trigger events that generate HL7 messages. In fact, there are over sixty different ADT trigger events, everything from cancel visit to delete record. But there is no reason to be alarmed, most of these trigger events are barely used. The 80-20 cornucopia keeps on giving. There are only a handful of ADT trigger events that are commonly used.

After Registration (A04), Admit (A01) and Discharge (A03), the next important ADT trigger event is A08 (Update Patient Information). This event is triggered whenever there is a change in the patient record. An "A O Eight" (that's how insiders pronounce A08) is a very heavily used ADT message.

Then there are other ADT trigger events worth knowing - transfer patient (A02), cancel admit (A11), cancel discharge (A13) and pre-admit (A05) are some of the examples.

One very important ADT trigger event is a merge event. This occurs in situations where, by mistake, two patient records have been created for the same person and the records have to be merged into one. Merge is a complex topic so we will address it separately in the next chapter.

Although each ADT trigger event generates a slightly different message, if you look at their message structure, you will notice that most ADT messages follow a common pattern.

After the control segments (MSH, EVN etc.) in the head of the message, the body starts with patient identification and related information (PID, PD1, NK1). This is followed by information about patient visit (PV1, PV2) and then you have all kind of other segments for allergy, diagnosis, procedure, insurance etc.

Of all the segments in ADT messages, PID (Patient Identification) and PV1 (Patient Visit) are the two most important data segments. These segments have a lot of fields between them but then again, the 80-20 rule is there to help. Only a small subset of fields in these segments is commonly used.

PID – Patient Identification Segment

The PID segment, as the name implies, carries information about the patient. It is one of the most frequently used segments and usually appears right after the control segments.

If you have a raw HL7 message and you want to find out the details of the patient, you look in the PID segment. This is where the patient's name, age, address and other demographic information is. There is another segment, PD1 (Patient Additional Demographic segment), for additional patient information but that segment is rarely used, if ever.

Let's parse the PID segment from our example message and look at its fields.

PID |1| |PAT416^^^HEALTH_ID| |SEBELUS^KANSAS| |194801150600|M| | |1 23SESAME ST^^TORONTO^ON^A1A2B2^CANADA| |(416) 888-8088| |ENGLISH |M| |PAT_AC_721914

PID-1:	1	- Sequence Number
PID-2:		
PID-3:	PAT416^^^HEALTH_ID	- Patient Identifier List
PID-4:		
PID-5:	SEBELUS^KANSAS	- Patient Name
PID-6:		
PID-7:	194801150600	- Date/Time of Birth
PID-8:	M	- Administrative Sex
PID-9:		
PID-10:		
PID-11:	123 SESAME ST^^TORONTO^ON^A1A 2B2^CANADA	- Address
PID-12:		
PID-13:	(416) 888-8088	- Phone Number – Home
PID-14:		
PID-15:	ENGLISH	- Primary Language
PID-16:	M	- Marital Status
PID-17:		
PID-18:	PAT_AC_721914	- Patient Account Number

PID segment has thirty nine fields but only two are mandatory, PID-3 (Patient ID) & PID-5 (Patient Name). All the other fields are optional. In the example segment we chose not to send any information after field eighteen. That's why the segment ends at PID-18 and implies that the remaining fields are empty.

PID-2 / PID-3 / PID-4: Patient Identifier Fields

Patient identifier is a very important field for healthcare applications. Usually, the field holds the MRN (medical record number), which is assigned to a patient at the time of registration. But there are other identifiers, such as billing account number, health card number or SSN that can be used to uniquely identify a patient.

There are three fields for patient identifier in the PID segment but only one, PID-3, is commonly used. Both PID-2 and PID-4 are deprecated, meaning they continue to exist only to support older versions of HL7. So you will see a value in PID-2 or 4 only for applications that were implemented in the past.

PID-3 is an important field. It is mandatory, so you can't leave this one empty. It is also a repeating field, meaning you can send multiple patient identifiers in PID-3. Of course, the identifiers will have to be separated by the repetition delimiter (~). An example would look something like this: PAT416^^^HEALTH_ID~999-99-9999^^^SSN.

Another thing to know about this field is that it is a compound field. There can be up to ten components in this field but we don't have to worry about that. Usually only component 1 (ID number) and 4 (Assigning Authority) are valued. That's why the value in the example looks like PAT416^^^HEALTH_ID. Component 1 (ID) is PAT416 and component 4 (assigning authority) is HEALTH_ID. This is the health card number of the patient.

PID-5: Patient Name

This is another mandatory field and a compound field that has way too many components. HL7 went overboard here. In addition to the usual first, middle and last names, they have defined components for prefix, suffix, degree, surname from partner… it's a long list.

In practice, we only populate the first three components, last name, first name and the middle name. In our example, we have only populated the first two, last and first name. It is not uncommon to add MD or whatever other degree a doctor has, to her name. Degree is the sixth component so there will be a lot of carets in the field, something like PAYNE^TRACY ^^^^MD.

PID-7 / PID-8: Patient Date & Time of Birth and Sex

Although these fields are optional, they almost always have a value. PID-7 (Date & Time of Birth) is in the TS (timestamp) format so the field value is sent as YYYYMMDDHHMM. If time is not available, only the date of birth (YYYYMMDD) is sent.

PID-8 represents the sex of the person. This field can only have one character. M is for male, F for female and U is for unknown. If sites want to define their own codes, they are free to do so but they will have to make sure that both the sending and the receiving systems are referring to the same set of codes. Otherwise, there will be a message failure and a big headache for implementers.

PID-11 / PID-13 / PID-14: Patient Address & Phone Number

These fields hold the contact information of the patient and are usually populated. All three are repeating fields so there can be multiple addresses and phone numbers.

In the example above, we also have values in the PID-15 (Primary Language) and PID-16 (Marital Status) fields. These fields are used to send additional demographic information about the patient. It all depends on the information collected by the healthcare facility and varies from one organization to the next.

Although this field is defined as optional, in my experience, this field is always populated. This is the financial/billing account number to which all expenses and charges for patient care are assigned. Even in jurisdictions where you have universal healthcare (like in Canada), the patient account number is populated and used for reporting and tracking expenses.

PV1 – Patient Visit Segment

This is another very important and extensively used data segment. It carries information about a patient's visit to a healthcare facility (which clinicians refer to as an encounter). Fields in this segment include type of patient (inpatient/outpatient), admitting doctor, date of admission, location of bed etc. In all, there are fifty two fields in this segment.

PV1 follows PID in the body of the message and is usually a mandatory segment. Let's parse PV1 from the example message and look at some of the important fields.

PV1 | 1 | O | ROOM10^BED12^OUTPATIENT | ELECTIVE | | | S21195^DRIKOFF^FRANCIS^^^DR^MD | | C90023^PAYNE^TRACY^^^DR^MD | SUR | | | | 1 | | | S21195^DRIKOFF^FRANCIS^^^DR^MD | | 37323 | SELF | | | | | | | | | | | | | | | | | | | | | | | 201310201500

PV1-1: 1	- Sequence Number
PV1-2: O	- Patient Class
PV1-3: ROOM10^BED12^OUTPATIENT	- Assigned Patient Location
PV1-4: ELECTIVE	- Admission Type
PV1-5:	
PV1-6:	
PV1-7: S21195^DRIKOFF^FRANCIS^^^DR^MD	- Attending Doctor
PV1-8:	- Referring Doctor
PV1-9: C90023^PAYNE^TRACY^^^DR^MD	- Consulting Doctor
PV1-10: SUR	- Hospital Service
PV1-11:	
PV1-12:	
PV1-13:	
PV1-14: 1	- Admit Source

```
PV1-15:
PV1-16:
PV1-17: S21195^DRIKOFF^FRANCIS^^^DR^MD        - Admitting Doctor
PV1-18:
PV1-19: 37323                                 - Visit Number
PV1-20: SELF                                  - Financial Class
PV1-21:
. . . .
PV1-44: 201310201500                          - Admit Date/Time
PV1-45:                                       - Discharge Date/Time
PV1-46:
. . . .
```

There is only one required field in this segment, PV1-2. But a number of other fields are usually populated. Fields populated in the example above are a good approximation of real life messages. There could also be one-off cases, where a rarely used field is populated.

Once, I came across a message where PV1-16 was valued and I didn't know what it was for. This field is for flagging VIP patients. It is there for health records of famous people and situations where the clinical staff might have more than a professional level of interest in the patient's medical history.

Remember when George Clooney had a motorcycle accident in New York and showed up at a local hospital. A lot of staff, especially women, were concerned about this patient in emergency, and were checking his records to make sure everything was all right. God knows why the media started screaming about breach of privacy.

PV1-2: Patient Class

This is the only required field in the PV1 segment. It contains a single letter, the code for the type of patient.

HL7 doesn't define a standard list of codes for the type of patient, although, there is a suggested list. A facility can use this suggested list or create its own custom list and share it with systems receiving the message.

Some commonly used codes are - I (Inpatient) for patients staying at the hospital, O (Outpatient) for patients who are just visiting for a consultation, dialysis or checkup but are not going to spend the night at the hospital and E (Emergency) for patients who came through the emergency department.

PV1-3 / PV1-6 / PV1-11: Patient Location

These fields contain a patient's location in the hospital. For outpatients, the field stays empty but for those who are inpatients, PV1-3 contains their current location in the hospital. If the patient was moved from another location, that prior location is in PV1-6 and if the patient is in a temporary bed, then that goes in PV1-11. Not all fields are always populated. Usually only PV1-3 is valued (current location).

These location fields are large and complicated. Each one is made up of eleven components and some of the components themselves are made up of subcomponents. However, the 80-20 rule is here to save us. Usually, only the first four components are valued. The first component is for the nursing station/unit, the second component is for the bed, the third component is for the room and the fourth one is for the facility/site. Together they are enough to pinpoint a patient's location in a hospital.

Patient location is an important field and used by many different clinical systems. I remember it being used in an Infection Control system to track the movement of patients who had antibiotic resistant infections (MRSA).

PV1-7 / PV1-8 / PV1-9 / PV1-17 / PV1-52: Doctors & Other Healthcare Providers

These fields contain the identifying information of doctors and other healthcare providers who are caring for or were involved in the care of the patient. PV1-7 is for the attending doctor, PV1-8 is for the referring doctor, PV1-9 is for doctor(s) consulted on the case, PV1-17 is for the doctor who admitted the patient (inpatient) and PV1-52 is for other healthcare providers like nurses and physiotherapist who are involved in the care of the patient.

These fields too are complicated compound fields but only a few components are used. The first component is the "ID Number" and it is used to uniquely identify the doctor. In Toronto, every doctor has a unique CPSO (College of Physicians and Surgeons of Ontario) number, which is often used as the ID number. But you can use a local or internal ID. As long as the number uniquely identifies a doctor, it is good to go.

Second to seventh components of the field are for the doctor's name. I would always populate the sixth and the seventh component with DR and MD respectively. After all, it takes years of toil to acquire those letters, so the least I could do was make sure it was part of the doctor's name.

The ninth component of the field is for the organization that assigned the "ID number" (first component) to the doctor. So if the CPSO number were being used then "CPSO" would go in this field.

PV1-19: Visit Number

Every patient visit to a healthcare facility is assigned a unique number called a visit number. This field holds that number. Before we answer why we need to assign a unique ID to every patient visit, you need to know how healthcare records are organized.

Healthcare records are organized in a hierarchy. At the top is the patient record, which is identified by the PID-3 (Patient Identifier) field. For each patient record, there could be one or more accounts, which are identified by an account number. These account numbers are found in the PID-18 (Patient Account Number) field. An account number is used for billing purposes to which all patient expenses are charged. Each account could have one or more patient visit (PV1-19) fields associated with it. So for a recurring visit like dialysis or physiotherapy, you can have a dedicated account to which all related visits are billed. And for one-off visits, such as an emergency, you have a separate account, both under the same patient record.

Now to the question why we need to assign a unique ID to every patient visit. A patient visit can lead to an order for a lab test, medication or some other service. By having a unique ID for every visit, it is easier to track orders by the visit number. A visit number also makes it easier to merge patient records.

This is an important field and it is almost always populated.

PV1-44 / PV1-45: Admit & Discharge Date/Time

These fields are used to capture the date and time of patient admittance and discharge. They are obviously used for inpatient visits but are sometimes also used for emergency patients and outpatients.

Order Message - Order Entry

It is time to turn our attention to another important group of HL7 messages called order messages. Their details are in Chapter 4 of the HL7 spec.

We call them order messages because messages in this group are used to order for supplies and services. It is only because of these messages that a system is able to electronically request medication from pharmacy, order a lab test, or request a patient's meal through the TV.

The HL7 spec defines an all-purpose order message type called a General Order message ORM^O01. This message type can be used to place different types of orders - medication, lab test, supply etc.

ORM^O01 has two very important segments - a Common Order Segment (ORC) and an Order Detail Segment. ORC is straightforward and we cover it in detail further below.

The Order Detail segment changes with the type of order being placed. Usually, it is an OBR (Observation Request segment), but for diet orders, it changes to ODS, for pharmacy, to RXO and for supply orders it is RQD. This is necessary to account for the unique information needed by different order types.

Things changed after version 2.3. Specialized order messages with a fixed message structure were created. These were OMG^O19 for clinical orders, OML^O21 for lab orders, OMD^O03 for diet orders, RDE^O11 for pharmacy orders, and so on.

It was recommended that these specialized order messages be used going forward, but ORM^O01 is such a widely used and entrenched message type that it continues to be the dominant and most important order message. If you learn about only ORM^O01 and OBR segment, it will take probably care of 80% of cases. For others, you can always turn back to the HL7 spec.

Before we take a closer look at segments ORC and OBR, let's get some important concepts out of the way.

Placer / Filler

Whenever an order is being placed for supplies and services, there are at least two systems involved in the transaction. The system that places the order and the system that fills the order (or provides the service). In HL7 parlance, a "Placer" is the system that places the order and a "Filler" is the system that fulfills the order or provides the services/supplies.

Suppose a physician enters an order for a blood test in the HIS (hospital information system), which converts that order into an HL7 message and sends it to the lab system. Here the HIS is the "placer" and the lab system, which fills the order, is the "filler".

It is not necessary for the placer and the filler to be separate systems; they can be the same system. For example, when an order is placed internally within a department.

Every time an order is created, the placer assigns it a unique number (Placer Order Number) before sending it to the filler. When the filler receives the order, it also assigns a unique number to the order (Filler Order Number) before any further processing is done. These numbers are very important and you will often need them for tracking and debugging order messages.

Order Control

Not every order goes through the same process. An order could be modified, cancelled, or put on hold. To account for all these different situations, ORC has an order control field (ORC-1) to communicate the current status of the order to the filler.

When the placer first creates an order, the status of the order is set to NW (New Order). Subsequently, if that order needs to be cancelled, the placer sends another order message with the same placer number as that of original order but the status is set to OC (Order Cancelled).

When the filler reads this second message, it will go ahead and cancel the order in its system. After cancellation, an acknowledgement with the order status CR (Cancelled as Requested) is sent back.

There are a lot of codes for order statuses and they are all there in Chapter 4 of the HL7 spec. Just to give you a taste, if the filler is not able to cancel the order, because maybe the test has already been performed, it will send back an acknowledgement with code UC (Unable to Cancel).

Segment Rules

The way ORC and Order Detail segments (OBR, ODS, RXO etc.) show up in a message can be confusing at times. But there are rules and if you know them, understanding the occurrence of these segments in a message becomes pretty straightforward.

For the sake of simplicity, we will use OBR for order detail segment.

Both ORC and OBR contain details of an order and there are many fields that are common between these two segments. A rule of thumb with these overlapping fields is that the value in ORC always overrides the value in OBR.

The best way to distinguish between these segments is to see ORC as the control segment and OBR as the data segment. Yes, they are both data segments but from the perspective of an order, ORC contains only the meta-data of an order, such as the status of the order, placer ID and filler ID. OBR, on the other hand, contains actual order details like what is being ordered and the details of the specimen (blood, urine etc.).

For a new order, you need an ORC/OBR pair to define the complete order. An ORC will spell out all the meta-data information and the OBR will contain the actual details of the order. However, for cancellation of an existing order, there is no need for an OBR. Just an ORC with the cancel (CA) status is enough.

There is another thing to keep in mind about order messages. A single HL7 message can have more than one order. It will just have more than one occurrence of an ORC/OBR pair or multiple ORC segments (for the case where more than one order is being cancelled).

Let's take a look at these segments now.

ORC – Common Order Segment

As mentioned earlier, an ORC segment is like the control segment of an order. It contains meta-data information about the order and is required in every order message. There are thirty fields in this segment but as you must have guessed, not everything is used.

ORC-1: Order Control

This is the only required field in the ORC segment and it is the most important field. It contains a two character "control code" to determine the status of the order. There are too many order control codes so I am just going to list the three categories that they are grouped under.

- Request from Placer (New Order - NW, Cancel Order - CA etc.)

- Acknowledgement from Filler (Order Accepted - OK, Cancelled as Requested - CR etc.)
- Notification from filler (Order Cancelled - OC, Unable to Cancel - UC etc.)

ORC-2 & ORC-3: Placer Order Number / Filler Order Number

ORC-2 (Placer Order Number) is the unique order number assigned by the placer of the order. This field is duplicated in the OBR segment (OBR-2). Either the ORC-2 or the OBR-2 should always be valued. Both of them cannot be empty. However, it is all right if both fields are populated, as long as they have the same value.

Similarly ORC-3 (Filler Order Number) is the unique order number assigned by the filler system. This field also has a duplicate in the OBR segment (OBR-3) and if it is not valued in the ORC, then it should be populated in the OBR.

ORC-7: Quantity/Timing

This field is not used anymore. Two new segments, TQ1 and TQ2 have taken over the role of defining the amount of medication, the frequency, the interval, the duration of administration and other details of an order.

These details become important for orders that involve activities like dispensing medication, making observations or collecting specimens.

The field is duplicated in the OBR segment (OBR-27).

ORC-12: Ordering Provider

This field contains the identifying information of the doctor/healthcare provider who placed the order. It is duplicated in the OBR segment (OBR-16) and should always be valued. If it is not present in the ORC, then it should definitely be there in the OBR segment.

These fields are optional. They contain the name, address and the phone number of the organization that placed the order. In other words, it contains the placer's contact information. These fields become relevant if the order is going to an external organization for processing, for example a private lab.

OBR – Order Detail Segment

There are many different flavors of order detail segment but the most common flavor is the OBR segment, which we will discuss here. It is used extensively in lab, radiology and other general order messages.

An OBR can be seen as a bridge segment between order and result messages. It is like the requisition form that goes with an order and comes back signed and filled with the result.

Some important fields in the OBR segment, from the placer point of view, are discussed below.

OBR-2 & OBR-3: Placer Order Number / Filler Order Number

As discussed earlier, OBR-2 (Placer Order Number) is a duplicate of the ORC-2 field. It holds the unique placer order number.

Similarly, OBR-3 (Filler Order Number) is the unique filler order number. It is a duplicate of the ORC-3 field.

OBR-4: Universal Service Identifier

This is the most important field in an order message. It is a required field and is mandatory because it holds the order code for whatever is being ordered. Without this code, filler won't know what the order is for.

OBR-7 & OBR-8: Observation Date/Time & Observation End Date/Time

These fields are relevant only in situations where a sample is being collected for an order (blood for a blood test) or an observation is being taken (body temperature, blood pressure, etc.). If the observation is taken over a period of time, then both OBR-7 and OBR-8 are populated. For cases that are a single point in time, such as getting a blood sample, then only OBR-7 is populated.

OBR-16: Ordering Provider

This field contains the identifying information of the doctor/healthcare provider who placed the order. It is a duplicate of ORC-12. The ordering provider information should always be present in an order message. If it is not present in the ORC segment, then it should definitely be valued in the OBR segment (OBR-16).

OBR segment has many other important and commonly used fields, such as OBR-22 (Result Status Change Date/Time) and OBR-25 (Result Status) but they are populated by the filler system and sent back with the result message. We discuss them in the result message.

Result Message – Observation Reporting

Result messages complete the communication loop between the placer and the filler applications. Earlier, we saw order messages being used by placers to electronically order for supplies and services. Many of these orders generate observations and results that the filler sends back to the placer. HL7 messages that carry these results are known as result messages.

Unlike orders, there is just one type of result message, ORU^R01 (Unsolicited Observation Message). This message type is used extensively for sending all kinds of results - lab results, patient observations, clinical reports and many others. There is another type of result message, OUL^R21, for automating lab systems, but I have never seen it used. We don't need to waste time on it.

The result message is covered in detail in Chapter 7 of the HL7 spec. It uses many of the same segments used by other message types (PID, PV1, ORC and OBR) but also defines a very important segment, the OBX (Observation/Result Segment). OBX segment is for the data in a result.

To get a good handle on the result message, you will need to know how results are organized in an HL7 message.

There are two ways in which a result/observation is reported through HL7. Text oriented reports (Narratives) and structured reports. Text oriented reports are formatted for human readability, so they are like a paper report with sentences and paragraphs. Structured reports, on the other hand, are meant for processing by the software. Here, the content of the report is distributed within the fields of the segments.

Both structured and text oriented reports are sent as ORU^R01 messages and follow the same message structure. The difference lies in the way OBX segments are populated. We will look at this difference when we discuss OBX segment.

Information in a result message is organized in a hierarchy. At the top of the hierarchy is the patient, which is represented by the PID segment. Each patient (PID) can have one or more result (OBR) in the message.

The OBR segment acts like the report header. It contains attributes common to all results in a set of tests. For those who don't know, lab tests & diagnostics are usually ordered as a set (or a battery or a panel) of many separate tests. When a doctor orders for the "vitals" of a patient, what she is asking for is the blood pressure, pulse and temperature of the patient. An order for an "electrolytes panel" means a blood test to measure the levels of sodium, potassium, chloride and carbon dioxide in the blood. All these are individual tests with their own results.

Individual test results are written in the OBX segment. One OBX segment holds the result for one test. So, a report for an "electrolytes panel" will have one header (OBR) followed by four OBX segments with the result for sodium, potassium, chloride and carbon dioxide levels in the blood.

To recap, at the top of the hierarchy is the PID segment representing the patient. Each PID can have one or more OBR segments, which is the header for a result set. Each OBR can have one or more OBX segments to capture the result of individual tests within an order.

The hierarchy doesn't end here. You can have an SPM (Specimen) segment under the OBX which itself can have OBXs under it. It does get complicated, but for an overview the PID-OBR-OBX hierarchy is good enough. This gives you the foothold to learn further.

Let's revisit the OBR segment now from the filler point of view.

OBR – Observation Request Segment

In a result message, an OBR segment serves as the report header for a test. A message can have multiple OBR segments, which just means that the message contains result for multiple order sets.

The OBR segment also acts like the turnaround document between the placer and the filler systems. The OBR in the order message contains fields populated by the ordering system (placer). The filler system uses the same OBR in the result message and populates additional filler fields and sends it back to the placer system.

A great example is the OBR-2/OBR-3 pair. The OBR-2 field holds the Placer ID, which is populated by the placer. The OBR-3 field is left empty when this order message is sent. When the filler responds either with an acknowledgement or the result, it populates the OBR-3 field with the Filler ID. Keep in mind that the result message also retains the OBR-2 value originally populated by the placer.

Some other fields commonly populated by the filler in an OBR segment include:

OBR-22: Date/Time of Result Report or Status Change

This field contains the date/time when the result became available or the status of the result changed. In other words, it represents the report date. Its counterpart, order date is populated by the placer in the OBR-6 field. Together, OBR-6 and OBR-22 can be used to calculate the turnaround time for an order.

OBR-24: Diagnostic Service ID

This is another commonly populated field in the result message. It represents the department that performed the test. The field contains a two or three letter code for various services. You will see values like MB (microbiology) or RAD (Radiology) in this field.

OBR-25: Result Status

This field holds the status of the result and is a required field in the OBR segment of the result message. It is an important field and if you are going to be working with result messages, this is one field you will be looking up frequently.

An important thing to keep in mind is that this field represents the status of a particular order set and not all the orders in a message. There could be result for multiple order sets in a result message and because of that there will be multiple OBR segments in the message. Each OBR-25 represents only the overall result status for its own order set.

OBX – Observation Result Segment

If the OBR segment is like the header of an ordered result then the OBX segment is the body of the result and holds the actual result data. Since one OBX segment can hold information only for a single observation, each OBR segment is generally associated with multiple OBX segments.

OBX-1: Set ID

Unlike other segments that have Set ID, it is a useful field in the OBX segment. It is the sequence number, which goes up by one for each successive OBX under an OBR. For OBXs associated with another OBR, the numbering restarts at one. This makes it easy to read a raw HL7 message.

OBX-2: Value Type

This field defines the data type of the result field (OBX-5). If the result is in the form of a narrative report, then the value in this field is always TX (code for text data). For structured reports, the value is usually CE (coded Entry) but it is possible that you may run into a different value.

OBX-3: Observation Identifier

If you remember, order sets and individual orders are represented by codes in an HL7 message. Usually LOINC codes are used to represent these orders.

The code for the overall order set is in the OBR-4 field but for individual orders that make up the order set, their codes are in the OBX-3 field. Each OBX-3 holds the code for one individual order.

OBX-5: Observation Value

This is the field that holds the result of the test. There is no limit on the length of this field. For narrative reports, this is where the sentences of the report go. Sentences are broken up into multiple OBX's so that it looks like a nicely formatted paragraph.

OBX-6: Units

This field identifies the unit of measurement for values in the OBX-5 field. If something is being reported as "1 ml" then "1" will be in the OBX-5 field and "ml" will be in the OBX-6 field.

OBX-11: Observation Result Status

This is a required field that is very important. It contains the code for the status of the result. This field is used extensively in managing records such as updating an old record, correcting a wrong result or marking a result as final.

In real life, you don't just get one message with the result of the ordered test. It is more typical to first receive a preliminary result. Then, maybe there is a correction to that test and a corrected result is sent. The lab may decide to run the tests again and issue a final result. All these results are sent one after the other. So, it is quite possible that an order will spawn two or three result messages.

A value of "P" in this field means the result is "Preliminary". "C" means the result is a "correction" of a previously reported result and "F" means this is the final value of the result.

10. Other Important Topics

We haven't touched on some important HL7 topics yet. But that is intentional. They are important to understanding HL7, but in my opinion, throwing a newcomer off the deep end is not the right way to teach someone to swim. Learning doesn't have to be a frightening experience.

So here at the deep end, let's first look at data types. Data types are an integral part of HL7. There is a whole chapter (2A) dedicated to them in the HL7 spec.

HL7 Data Type

In HL7 you have your usual data types such as text and numeric but then you also have data types for name, address, visiting hours, frequency of medication and other values that are not normally considered a data type.

If you are thinking that the data type for name should be just text, then you do have a point. However, in HL7, data types take on a bigger role. They are used to gain a very fine control over the structure of a field - how it is defined, and to impose restrictions on its content. For regular data types, you only have restriction on the type of value (Boolean, text or numeric). With HL7, the restrictions go way beyond just the type of value. There are restrictions on the length, on how the content is organized, when a value has to be present etc.

Remember the building blocks of a message? A message is a collection of segments, which is a collection of fields, which is a collection of components and so on. Data types come into play at the field level. Whether a field has components and sub-components depends entirely on the data type of that field. If a data type has five components and two of those components are further made up of subcomponents, then the field inherits that property. It can be said that the field has five components and two of those have subcomponents.

If you look at the attribute table of any segment, the third column with the heading DT is the data type column. It contains the data type code for fields in that segment. The codes are usually two or three characters in length and are always in uppercase.

Chapter 2A of the specification document defines all the data types in HL7. For details of a particular data type, you will need to look in Chapter 2A, where they are listed in the alphabetical order.

I consider it highly unlikely but if you do spend time browsing Chapter 2A, you will notice that some data types are very simple. They have just one component. These are the familiar data types - ST (String), NM (Numeric), TX (Text) etc. Others data types use these basic types to form more complex types and then you have the scary ones which are made up of both simple and complex data types. They are the poster children for what scares people away from HL7.

I like to organize data types into basic, intermediate and complex categories. Basic is the simplest data type with just one component. Then you have the intermediate types with multiple components of basic type and finally, there is the complex data type, which is a mix of both basic and intermediate types.

Let's look at an example of each.

NM – Numeric Data Type

HL7 component Table - NM – Numeric

SEQ	LEN	DT	OPT	TBL#	Component Name
	16				Numeric

Source: HL7 Specification Document v2.5, Chapter 2A

This is an example of a basic data type. A field with this data type can only have numeric values with a maximum length of sixteen characters. It also allows a leading sign (+/-) and a decimal point within the value. (Examples: 21 and +33.90).

NR – Numeric Range Data Type

HL7 component Table - NR – Numeric Range

SEQ	LEN	DT	OPT	TBL#	Component Name
1	16	NM	O		Low Value
2	16	NM	O		High Value

Source: HL7 Specification Document v2.5, Chapter 2A

This is an intermediate level data type. It has two components, both of which are basic NM data types. A field with this type defines a range of value by specifying the lowest possible and the highest possible value in the range.

As you can see in the table, the first component is always the low value and both components are optional. For example if a field looks like 70^110 then the value ranges from a low of 70 to a high of 110.

PTA – Policy type and amount

HL7 Component Table – PTA – Policy Type and Amount

SEQ	LEN	DT	OPT	TBL#	Component Name
1	5	IS	R	147	Policy Type
2	9	IS	O	193	Amount Class
3	16	NM	B		Money or Percentage Quantity
4	23	MOP	R		Money or Percentage

Source: HL7 Specification Document v2.5, Chapter 2A

This is an example of a complex data type. There are multiple components where some have their own components (MOP). A couple of components also have restrictions on the value. Look at column TBL#. The first two components can only have the values listed in those tables.

But I am not giving you a true picture of complex data types with this example. Many of them, like XCN and XAD, are truly monstrous and contain tens of components and sub-components.

Using Data Types

So far we have only dealt with the theory behind data types. In practice, we don't deal with all this complexity. Let's take one complex data type and see how it is really used in a real world application.

Imagine you are mapping the PID segment for a message. So now you have to get all the patient related information mapped out. When you come to the PID-5 field, you see that it's the patient name field and the data type is XPN. This means the patient's name has to be written according to XPN data type requirements. You cannot just drop the name as one long string. The receiving system will reject the message.

So how do you map the patient's name? This information will be in the interface spec and interface specs are based on HL7 specs. So more often than not, data types are defined exactly accordingly to HL7 spec. Assuming that is the case, lets head to Chapter 2A and scroll down to where the component table for the XPN data type is defined.

HL7 Component Table – XPN – Extended Person Name

SEQ	LEN	DT	OPT	TBL#	Component Name
1	194	FN	O		Family Name
2	30	ST	O		Given Name
3	30	ST	O		Second and Further Given Names or Initials
4	20	ST	O		Suffix (e.g. JR or III)
5	20	ST	O		Prefix (e.g. DR)
6	6	IS	B	0360	Degree (e.g. MD)
7	1	ID	O	0200	Name Type Code
8	1	ID	O	0465	Name Representation Code
9	483	CE	O	0448	Name Context
10	53	DR	B		Name Validity Range
11	1	ID	O	0444	Name Assembly Order
12	26	TS	O		Effective Date
13	26	TS	O		Expiration Date
14	199	ST	O		Professional Suffix

Source: HL7 Specification Document v2.5, Chapter 2A

What we have here is a data type with fourteen components. A look at the fourth column (OPT), which defines whether a component is required or optional, tells us that everything is optional. (O is optional and B is backward compatibility/previous version, ignore B). This is what makes life easy.

If the name of the patient is "Tommy Boy" then all you will need to populate are the first two components as Boy^Tommy. You can ignore the rest.

Why is that? Because XPN data type requires the first component to be the family name. Then you have a component separator ^ followed by the given name in the second component. That's why Tommy Boy's name is written as Boy^Tommy.

By leaving out the rest of the components in the name field, we are indicating that the remaining components are empty.

Let's add a little twist to the name. Say, Tommy Boy's full name is "Tommy Boy Jr.". Now there is a suffix in the name and if you refer to the table above, suffix should go in the fourth component. In this case, the name will be written as Boy^Tommy^^Jr. There are two carets side by side (^^) in this name. This is to indicate that the third component is empty and "Jr." is the value in the fourth component.

Do you see now why I said you don't have to deal with all the complexity? Most names are simple and that means only the first three or four components are populated and we ignore the rest. The same is true for other data types. If you do come across an unfamiliar component populated in a field, a quick visit to Chapter 2A will solve the problem.

Also, the 80-20 rule works very well with HL7 data types. Only a handful of data types are commonly used. We can safely ignore the vast majority. Here are a few commonly used examples.

Coded Element (CE)

This is a very common data type in HL7, but to the uninitiated, it means nothing. A field with this data type can only have a coded value. An example would be LOINC code for lab result.

When lab tests are reported electronically, they don't use long descriptive sentences to report their findings. Instead, alphanumeric codes are used to represent the type of test. It is these codes along with the result values that are sent across in an HL7 message. A field with a CE data type means it can only contain valid codes defined by a coding system (like LOINC). You can also define your own local codes and use that in a CE field.

There are a couple of variations to this data type. CNE (Coded with No Exception) data type means the field can only have those codes that are defined by the coding system. CWE (Coded With Exception), on the other hand, allows codes to be defined locally in order to extend the coding system.

Coded Value (ID – for HL7 tables; IS – for user tables)

Whenever you come across a field with an ID or IS data type, it means there is a table linked to this field. You can find the table number in the attribute table for that data type. It is a four digit number under the TBL# column. In HL7, every table is assigned a unique four digit table number.

The reason we have tables is because there are many fields where it is necessary to define a standard set of values. For example, consider the case of the "sex" field. We can say that valid values in this field are male, female and unknown. But if the text is not standardized, it will lead to all kinds of variations. Guy and gal, for example.

For some of the fields, HL7 sets the values and defines the table. An example is Table 0003, which contains a list of all valid event codes. The EVN-1 field can only take values from this table.

For others, HL7 defines a suggested list of values in a table. It is left to the sites to decide if they want to use those values, modify them or create their own values. Table 0001 (Administrative Sex) is a good example.

And finally, there are fields like "Pre-Admit Test Indicator" (PV1-12) where the values can only be defined locally. HL7 only assigns the table number (0087).

Merge Messages

Merge messages are a subset of ADT that deal specifically with merging patient records in a database. These messages are for record housekeeping but that should not lull you into thinking that they are not important. Far from it. They are used often and chances are high that you will encounter them someday. Any HL7 expert worth his/her salt should understand merge. In fact, that is how we used to test the level of expertise of a new colleague.

There are three kinds of operations where merge messages are used: merging the content of two records into one, moving a child record from one place to another and changing the ID of a record.

Before we go any further, let's recap how health records are organized. At the very top is the person record. A person could be a patient, a relative, a doctor, etc. If the person is a patient, then the patient record sits under the person record. Each patient record can have one or more account records to track resources used (for example, an account for recurring dialysis visits and a separate one for an emergency visit). Each account can have one or more patient visit records linked to it. Visually this is what the hierarchy will look like.

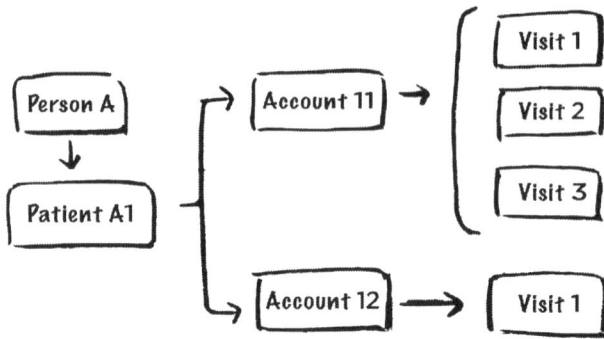

There are situations where this neat hierarchy of records gets tangled up. Consider the case of Mr. Rocky Racoon. He pays a visit to the hospital with a dislocated shoulder. The registration clerk looks up the hospital system to see if he has a record. None are found, so a new patient record is created for Rocky. This is where the problem starts. Rocky has been to that hospital before and has an existing patient record. The registration clerk searched for his name incorrectly even though Rocky told him specifically that he spells his last name with a single c - Racoon and not Raccoon. Of course, the system did not find his name, and now, there are two patient records for Rocky. If only we could take the human factor out!

This is a case of multiple records for the same person and it is resolved by merging the new record with Rocky's earlier patient record. Basically, it means moving the account and visit records from under the new patient record to the old patient record and deleting the new record.

A different situation could be that there is another guy Rocky Raccoon and he does spell his name with a double c. In that case, our Rocky's account and visit information is attached to the wrong patient record. This is resolved by moving the account and visit records to the correct patient record. This is a move operation.

Finally, there is the situation of an incorrect identifier assigned to a record. This doesn't happen anymore because identifiers are assigned automatically by the systems. But back in the days when identifiers were manually created, this was a real issue. Say, a hospital required all patient numbers to be seven characters in length and start with an alphabet. A new employee, not knowing any better, creates a record where patient number is only five characters in length and doesn't start with an alphabet. This will be a change operation.

Now that we understand what is involved in a merge operation, let's see how HL7 messages facilitate this. Altogether, eighteen different trigger events are defined for merge, move and change operations, half of those are just legacy triggers. HL7 is a lot like the DNA, there are many base pairs that do nothing but probably were useful at some point during evolution.

Trigger events A18, A30, A34, A35, A36, A39, A46 and A48 are there to maintain backward compatibility. Of the rest, three trigger events are for merge operation (A40, A41 & A42), three for move (A43, A44 & A45) and the remaining four for change operation (A47, A49, A50 & A51). Merge operations are the most important and frequently used, so we will take a closer look at them.

There are three different merge messages - event A40 is for merging at the patient record level, A41 is for merging at the account level and A42 is for merging at the visit level.

All three have similar message structures and the most important segment in these messages is the merge segment (MRG). It has three important fields: MRG-1 (prior patient ID), MRG-3 (prior account number) and MRG-5 (prior visit number). These fields identify records that have to be merged.

This is how the merge process works.

Every merge message has a PID and an MRG segment (and a PV1 segment if the merge is at the visit level). Their content includes the identifiers of the records to be merged.

The record, which will continue to exist, is called the surviving record and its identifier is in the PID segment. The record that will be merged is the non-surviving (or prior) record and its identifier is in the MRG segment.

For a merge at the patient record level, the surviving patient ID is in the PID-3 field and the non-surviving ID is in the MRG-1 field. Other MRG fields stay empty. This tells the receiving application to keep the patient ID in PID-3 and move records under MRG-1 to PID-3. How records are moved is decided by the receiving application. This is a database operation and HL7 leaves it at the discretion of the implementers.

Similarly, if two patient accounts are being merged then the surviving account number goes in PID-18 and the non-surviving account number goes in MRG-3. For merges at the visit level, the surviving visit number goes in PV1-19 and the non-surviving visit number goes in MRG-5.

Query Messages

Although not as widely used, HL7 query messages play an important role in clinical system communication. They could be used by an ancillary system to confirm the identity of a doctor with the provider registry or a reporting application could use them to request for a list of patients visiting emergency between midnight and 8:00 AM.

The standard only defines the broad framework for implementing query using HL7 messages. Details, like the information to be shared and the parameters to be supplied, are left to the implementers to decide.

Queries are implemented as a request/response message pair. The requesting system sends an HL7 message to the source system with search parameters. The source system uses these parameters to look for the information in its database and sends back another HL7 message with the information (or an error message if nothing was found).

Query messages have been changing and evolving over the years, and currently the standard defines three ways that a requestor can ask for information and three ways that a source can provide the information back to the requestor.

First, lets look at ways to ask for the information (defining a query). A requesting system can create a query as a query by parameter (QBP), a query by example (QBE) or a complex expression query (QSC).

All three options use a segment called parameter definition segment (QPD), to supply the details of the query. For those familiar with databases, the process is similar to invoking a stored procedure by supplying the procedure name and parameters. For those unfamiliar, a stored procedure is a pre-defined query with a name. They are useful for frequently used queries where instead of defining the query again and again, you define it once, give it a short name, and whenever you need to run it, you just call the short name with parameters.

Here is an example. Suppose all patient demographic records are stored in a table called pt_dem. If you want a list of patients by their marital status, then you define a query - "get all last name and first name from pt_dem table where marital status is = x". The marital status field (x) is the parameter that is supplied with the query. This query can be saved as a stored procedure. You can give it a name, for example *patient_list_by_marital_status*, and whenever you want a list of patients by marital status, you run this query.

Now, do you want a list of patients who are single? No problem. Call *patient_list_by_marital_status* where x=single. Simple!

Query by Parameter (QBP)
This is the simplest method. The message supplies the query name and parameters in the QPD segment. The system invokes the query and plugs in the parameter, for example,

QPD I Z05^patient_list_by_marital_status I Isingle

Query by Example (QBE)

This method is similar to QBP with the difference that the parameters are not sent in a QPD segment. They are sent in their respective segment fields. So instead of sending the value "single" in a QPD segment, a PID segment will be added to the message and PID-16, which is the marital status field, will be populated with the value S (for single). For example,

QPD | Z05^patient_list_by_marital_status | |
PID | | | | | | | | | | | | | | | | | | |S

The advantage of this method is that systems don't have to communicate what the parameter is. In the first method, the receiving system has to be told beforehand that QPD-3 is the field for marital status. Otherwise, it won't know what the value is for and the situation gets worse if there are multiple parameters.

In the case of QBE, there is no need for any of this. PID-16 is the marital status field defined by HL7. This is universally known and the receiving system uses this knowledge to intelligently extract the parameter from the message.

Complex Expression Query (QSC)

This is the most complex of the three methods. In this case, the requesting system defines the exact search criteria of the query as an expression similar to database language SQL. The field, QPD-3, holds the expression, but the data type of QPD-3 in this case is QSC (Query Selection Criteria).

The QSC data type has four components: field name, operator, value and relational conjunction. These four components are used to form the search expression that goes in the QPD-3 field. For our query, the field is PID-16 (marital status), the operator is equal (EQ) and the value is "single". There are no relational conjunctions (AND, OR, etc.) therefore the query segment will look something like this:

QPD | Z05^patient_list_by_marital_status | | @PID.16^EQ^Single |

Each method has its advantages and disadvantages. If you want something simple and straightforward to implement, you go with a QBP. On the other hand, a QSC is best suited for situations that require a lot of flexibility and the ability to define complex queries and extract very specific information.

Now, let's look at three ways to send the information back to the requesting system. The options are – Tabular, Display and Segment Pattern formats.

Tabular format is a simple and easy to process option. Data is returned as a table in the message. Column headers go in the RDF (Table Row Definition) segment and rows go in repeating RDT (Table Row Data) segments. This makes it very easy for the receiving system to parse the segments and reconstruct the table.

Display format is similar to Tabular but is also pre-formatted for human readability. It can be easily displayed on a screen or printed out. The result comes across as repeating DSP (Display Data) segments in the response message. The DSP-3 field holds the pre-formatted data, which can be sent directly to a printer or a computer screen for display.

Segment Pattern format is different. It sends the result through standard HL7 segments. So if a query is for patient records, those records are returned as PID segments in the response message. If there are multiple records, then multiple PID segments are returned.

The Segment Pattern format is great for complex and large results. For example, a lab result where entire segment groups (OBR, OBX etc.) are returned in the result message. But cases where only a few fields are needed, this format will add unnecessary parsing and processing overhead.

We are not going to discuss the segments involved in query messages. There is a lot to learn, especially if you are working with queries. The discussion here is only a precursor for further reading on this topic in Chapter 5 of the HL7 spec. In the spec you will also discover that there are many other message types like financial transaction, scheduling etc. that we didn't discuss in this book.

This book is only an attempt to pry open the HL7 doors for you. And the topics we have discussed so far, more than do the job. So this is good place to call it a day for this introductory book. I hope it was a good read and you enjoyed it.

I don't know what motivated you to read this book. If it was just to get familiar with the subject, then you are done. You can check it off your "to do" list and enjoy that satisfying feeling. On the other hand, if this is your first step towards mastering the subject, then you are all set to step into the brave new world of HL7 and make it your own.

Welcome to the world of HL7! ☺

Index

HL7Book.com

Please visit the companion website to provide your
feedback and suggestions.

Did you spot a typo? Or an error? Please drop me a line through
the feedback page. I'll appreciate it.

Printed in Great Britain
by Amazon